**David Eldridge, Robert Holman and
Simon Stephens**

A Thousand Stars Explode in the Sky

WITHDRAWN FROM
THE LIBRARY

UNIVERSITY OF
WINCHESTER

UNIVERSITY OF WINCHESTER
LIBRARY

Methuen Drama

Published by Methuen Drama 2010

Methuen Drama, an imprint of Bloomsbury Publishing Plc

3 5 7 9 10 8 6 4

Methuen Drama
Bloomsbury Publishing Plc
50 Bedford Square
London WC1B 3DP
www.methuendrama.com

Copyright © David Eldridge, Robert
Holman and Simon Stephens 2010

David Eldridge, Robert Holman and Simon Stephens have
asserted their rights under the Copyright, Designs and
Patents Act, 1988, to be identified as the authors of this work

ISBN 978 1 408 13146 6

A CIP catalogue record for this book is available from
the British Library

Available in the USA from Bloomsbury Academic & Professional,
175 Fifth Avenue/3rd Floor, New York, NY 10010.
www.BloomsburyAcademicUSA.com

Typeset by MPS Limited, a Macmillan Company
Printed and bound in Great Britain by
CPI Cox & Wyman, Reading, Berkshire

Caution
All rights whatsoever in this play are strictly reserved and application for
performance etc. should be made before rehearsals begin to Casarotto Ramsay
and Associates Limited, Waverley House, 7–12 Noel Street, London W1F 8GQ.
No performance may be given unless a licence has been obtained.

No part of this publication may be reproduced in any form or by any means –
graphic, electronic or mechanical, including information storage and retrieval
systems – without the written permission of Bloomsbury Publishing Plc.

This book is produced using paper that is made from wood grown in managed,
sustainable forests. It is natural, renewable and recyclable. The logging and
manufacturing processes conform to the environmental regulations of the
country of origin.

A Thousand Stars Explode in the Sky

UNIVERSITY OF WINCHESTER

03786315	822 91/ELD

A Thousand Stars Explode in the Sky was first performed at the Lyric Hammersmith, London, on 7 May 2010. The cast was as follows:

Edward Benton	Andrew Sheridan
Harriet Benton	Tanya Moodie
Jake Benton	Alan Williams
James Benton	Pearce Quigley
Margaret Benton	Ann Mitchell
Nicola Benton	Kirsty Bushell
Philip Benton	Harry McEntire
Roy Benton	Rupert Simonian
William Benton	Nigel Cooke
Dorrity Porter	Lisa Diveney
Karl Steiner	Tom Mothersdale

Director   Sean Holmes
Designer   Jon Bausor
Sound Designer   Nick Manning

The play was written with the support of The Peggy Ramsay Foundation.

Characters

James Benton, *thirty-eight*
William Benton, *fifty*
Jake Benton, *forty-eight*
Nicola Benton, *thirty-one*
Roy Benton, *fifteen*
Philip Benton, *fourteen*
Harriet Benton, *thirty-seven*
Margaret Benton, *seventy-one*
Edward Benton, *twenty-eight*
Dorrity Porter, *nineteen*
Karl Steiner, *sixteen*

Scene One

A single room in James Cook Memorial Hospital in Middlesbrough.
It is Friday morning.
William *is sitting on the edge of the bed. He is fifty years old. He is*
wearing a hospital gown, tied at the back, and a watch with a
leather strap.
James *is some distance away. He is thirty-eight years old. He has a*
paperback book in the back pocket of his jeans.

William Is this the end of the world? The experts have
said why it's going to happen. They haven't said what it's
going to feel like.

William *gathers strength. He looks at his brother.*

You're the historian. I think we live in an age of experts. We
must trust them until they're proved wrong.

He picks up a newspaper.

A cosmic string is going to tear the Universe into a thousand
pieces. It's a pearl necklace of black holes. It will slice
through everything we know like a cheese cutter. I looked at
the heavens as a child. You weren't born. The greatness of it
all. I've always known I was insignificant. The world is a tiny
place. We're not important. A thousand pieces seems
survivable to me.

A powerful shaft of sunlight comes in though the window and lights
William *on the bed. He looks at his brother.*

As I've got older you've all become more important. You
know I'm dying.

James Yes.

William The cancer has spread from my colon into my hip.

James Yes.

William I'm having a hip replacement this afternoon.

James I know.

William   I've the same chance between life and death. The surgery carries with it a significant risk. I might die later today.

James   Yes.

William   I've had a wire umbrella put into my heart. It's called a Cava Filter. It looked a bit like the cosmic string that's been all over the news. It's a new type. Dr Ali was reading the instructions as he put it in. It went through a vein in my groin. It's to stop blood clots when they do my hip.

James   I know.

William   Have you come from Twickenham?

James   Yes.

William   This morning?

James   Yes. The train to Darlington. And then the Poverty Train to Middlesbrough.

Silence.

William *folds the newspaper and puts it beside him on the bed.*

William   Did Harriet come with you?

James   No.

William   I see. Where's Mum?

James   She's outside. With Philip. There's a soft drinks machine, and a big screen with the news.

William   Will you go and tell her that I hope I die.

William *looks at his brother.*

I don't want to live this afternoon.

James *walks away.*

William   You were always a coward. You were never trustworthy. The little liar that you were. Always the spoilt one, James. The one Mum cared for for some reason. The delicate one, when we were all delicate really.

James   I didn't make friends.

William   You lived by your silence.

A slight pause.

I don't want your silence now.

James *looks at his brother.*

James   No.

William   I feel sorry for Harriet. She must hate you.

James   She loves me. She does what I want.

William   I don't know why.

Philip *comes into the room. He is fourteen years old. He is plump with three chins, and he is wearing his school uniform. He has a can of soft drink.*

Philip   There's a date and it's going to be in three weeks. NASA have a nuclear telescope buried miles and miles beneath the Antarctic called AMANDA. They've clarified the images. The cosmic string is moving towards us faster than they thought. If I'd invented a nuclear telescope it wouldn't have been a girl. Mine would have been called HENRIK.

William   It's an acronym.

Philip   I thought I'd better tell you we're all definitely going to die.

A pause.

Pardon me for breathing. I won't in future.

William   When?

Philip   In three weeks. Three weeks tomorrow. Saturday. At midnight.

Philip *drinks from the can.* **William** *holds out his hand.* **Philip** *gives him the can.*

You're not supposed to drink anything.

William *changes his mind. He gives the can back to* **Philip**.

You'd only be stealing. I paid for it with my own money.

Silence.
Philip *sits on the bed beside* **William**.
A pause.

James   Go to Mum, Philip.

Philip   She doesn't like me, so what's the point.

Philip *drinks from the can. He holds out his hand and offers the can to* **James**. **James** *takes it. He drinks.*

James   On the way here I was thinking about us. If I see a family today with five boys I always think about us. I want to say there was a family on the train, but there wasn't. Just five Geordie men with a lot of cheese. They'd been to Paris and brought back all these different cheeses. All the carriage had some. It was like a party. People were hysterically drunk on Saint Agur and Blue Brie.

A slight pause.

I was thinking about Jake. I remember the absolute silence when he got his girlfriend pregnant. I was six. I didn't know what it was. I know it hurt.

He looks at **William**.

You should have explained it to me, but you didn't. I remember Edward running away and coming to stay with me in Exeter, when I was at college. You should have helped him, but you didn't.

A slight pause.

He was nine. He was a young boy. I did my very best. It wasn't fair.

He drinks from the can.

Mum couldn't deal with him, that's all. Five brothers. She's never been able to deal with any of us. Go to her, Philip.

Philip No. I won't.

Silence.
William *gathers strength. He puts his arm on the bed and tries to lift himself up.* **Philip** *tries to help him.* **William** *pushes him away and manages to stand unaided for a moment.*

William Get out of this room immediately. Go on, get out.

James No. Not now.

William *reaches for his stick.* **Philip** *gives it to him.*

James I was thinking about when Grandma Dorrity died. And we went to the funeral in Stockport. I had to wear my tatty school blazer, with the school badge and everything. You wouldn't do it now. No one would. Mum thinks we're closer than we are.

William Yes.

James She wanted me to see you before you died. Why are you jealous of me?

William Am I?

James Yes, you are.

William You were lucky. You got away. You were bright. You were clever. It's not got you very far.

James It's got me further than Jake. It's got me further than you.

William Yes, it has.

James When I was a boy – why didn't you like me?

A slight pause.

William I don't know. I wasn't aware that I didn't like you.

James   Why didn't you like Edward?

William   I didn't want children. You should understand that.

James   It was not your choice.

William   No.

James   It was your responsibility. We all have the same mother.

A slight pause.

William   I didn't know you felt so strongly.

James *is unable to control one of his legs. It shakes a little.*

James   This is nothing compared to what I really feel.

A slight pause.

Philip   Was I born when Grandma Dorrity died?

James   No, you didn't know her.

Philip   Was she Mum's mother?

James   Yes.

A slight pause.

Philip   It's not Mum's fault. She's just embarrassed sometimes. I sometimes wonder if she shouldn't have had five girls.

He looks at **James**.

William's been good to me, James. I think you should be extremely quiet.

William   Where is Edward, d'you know?

James   No. I've absolutely no idea.

William   You were close to him at one time, weren't you.

James   Yes. He's somewhere in the world.

William   We must find him.

James   What?

William   We must find him.

James   Why?

William   You must find him. I can't. How can I find him?
You two must find him.

A slight pause.

James   I was thinking about the farm. There was a heron
on the platform at York. As the train was in the station, in
those few minutes, I watched it die. D'you remember the
heron we had as a pet? They take to the first thing they see,
which was Mum's skirt. It followed her everywhere. Then
one day, it just flew off.

A slight pause.

And the pet pig at Mill Farm. One pig amongst hundreds of
pigs. She was meant to teach you about farming, and all we
little ones did was ride around on her back. Then when she
had piglets we wouldn't let Mum or Dad send them for
slaughter, since they all had names and were friends.

William   Yes. They were slaughtered.

James   I know.

A slight pause.

Mum used to swear on the farm. The first time I heard her
swear I was amazed. I can't say what she said because it
would amaze you, about me. The f word. I'm a different
person now. You're the same person, William.

A slight pause.

William   Have you had your colonoscopy?

James   Yes. I had three pre-cancerous polyps which
they've removed. In a way, you've given me life. In other
circumstances I might be grateful. Absolutely everything
in the world is altered.

William   Yes.

A slight pause.

Did you know I nearly killed Jake?

William *falls to the floor.*
Philip *looks at* **James**.

Leave me.

William *gathers strength. He picks himself up. He uses the stick. He leans on it.*

It was the year I went to Cirencester.

Philip *gets up to help him.*

Stop your continual interference, Philip.

Philip *sits on the bed.*

It was the year I had at agricultural college. I think I would be eighteen. I can't remember. It's all gone for the moment. Jake would be sixteen. It was just before he got his girlfriend pregnant and the silence you talked about. He came to Cirencester. We shared my room for a week. I think it was the Ford Zodiac – it was the one with the long front seat like a settee. I drove like crazy. It was madness. I put it in a ditch on purpose. Jake knew. He went though the windscreen. It was the year Grandma Dorrity came from Stockport, when she and Granddad were troubled yet again. Dorrity took Jake's room for some reason. Jake came to me. I tried to kill him. You never knew because Mum didn't want you to know. You would be six or seven.

A slight pause.

I don't want this operation this afternoon. I don't want to die. I want to live.

He looks at one brother.

Philip, the pressure from you is intolerable.

He looks at his other brother.

I want us all to die together. I want you to find Edward. I know I can make it. I'm not going to have the operation.

Dr Ali can spend the time with his children. They can go and fly their kites. In three weeks' time I want to watch the sky fall in, and I want to watch it with you. I want the five of us to be together. I want to watch it with Mum. I will be there. I promise you that. When I die I want the whole world to die with me.

Scene Two

The balcony outside the Balcony Bar at Piccadilly Station in Manchester.
It is early the following Sunday morning.
There is a round, metal table, but no stools.
Jake *is standing, looking down at the platforms. He is forty-eight years old.*
Nicola *is with him. She is thirty-one years old. She has an orange in her hand and a bag at her feet.*
Roy *is playing with a Tamogochi. He is fifteen years old.*
Nicola *looks at her son and then at her father.*

Nicola   Jake, is he all right?

Jake   He's completely fine. He's just a little bit unnerved by seeing you again.

Nicola   Is that a Tamogochi? Can I see it, Roy?

Roy *does not look up.*

He's grown tall, hasn't he? You've grown big, you know.

Jake   It's been six years since you've seen him.

Nicola   Do you think he looks like me?

Jake *looks out at the station.*

Do you think he looks more like me than he did six years ago? I brought you here when you were a baby.

A train pulls out of the platform. **Nicola** *and* **Jake** *watch it go.*

I've always liked Piccadilly Station. I like this view.

Nicola *takes a kitchen knife from her inside pocket and dissects the orange.*

I like this bar. I like the way they've screwed the tables to the floor. I like it. Someone knows I steal them. I like train stations as a whole really. I like train travel. It's my favourite means of transport.

She eats a quarter of her orange and sucks the flesh off the skin. She puts the peel into her pocket.

When you travel by train you get to see the scope of the entire country.

Jake   We can't stay here.

Nicola   Have you got any money?

Jake   Have I what?

Nicola   I need about a thousand pounds. That might be a massive exaggeration by the way. Or I might need two thousand. Would you like a piece of my orange, Roy?

Roy   No, thank you.

Nicola   I don't blame you. When I was fifteen I didn't eat oranges either – and I still think you should never trust a marrow. When I was fifteen I thought to myself – I'm going to be the Queen of the world with a coronation robe made of peacock feathers.

Jake   What on earth do you need money for?

Nicola   I'd rather not tell you, it's private if you don't mind.

Nicola *eats another segment of her orange and sucks the flesh off the skin. She puts the peel into her pocket.*

Jake   Are you in trouble?

Nicola   I thought I saw you yesterday. That's a bit berserk because I was in London yesterday and you weren't, were you?

A slight pause.

Or were you?

Roy *laughs.* **Nicola** *laughs.*

I thought I saw you at the park at the bottom of my street. You were eating a packet of chips. Did you eat a packet of chips yesterday?

Roy   I don't remember.

Nicola   I completely bet you did. I like the countryside best, I think. I love living in London. I prefer it to here by a million miles. But I do like going to the countryside. That's how I think I'm going to spend the rest of my life and I can hardly wait. Some people are freaking me out. They're converting to Buddhism and Zoroastrianism and everything, but I've noticed that Scientologists aren't very popular. I'm going to get on a train and I'm going to go walking around, all over the place, in my boots. What are you going to do, Jake?

A slight pause.

What are you going to do with the rest of your short life?

Jake *looks at her.*

Jake   I think I might go and see Uncle William at the farm.

Nicola   And what's that got to do with the price of eggs?

A slight pause.
Nicola *turns to* **Roy.**

Are you all right?

Roy *is playing with the Tamogochi.*
Nicola *turns to* **Jake.**

I like walking. And I do like Kendal Mint Cake. Have you seen my boots?

She lifts her foot and puts it on the table to show off her boot.

These are the best running away boots in the world.

Roy *looks up.*

UNIVERSITY OF WINCHESTER
LIBRARY

Roy They're Mephisto. They're expensive.

Roy smiles. He looks at **Jake**. *Roy taps his knuckles on* **Jake**'s *forehead.*

Knock knock.

Jake Nicola, put your foot down.

Nicola glares at him. She takes her foot off the table.

Nicola I'm really, really hungry, actually. Aren't you, Roy?

Roy is playing with the Tamogochi.
Nicola *moves her head down towards her son's fingers.*

He could give us five pounds for a mega double bacon mushroom Swiss burger if anyone's serving.

Jake Was that the only reason that you wanted to see me, Nicola, now?

Nicola Would it matter if it was?

Silence.
Nicola *tickles* **Roy**'s *tummy.*
Roy *smiles. He will not laugh.*
Nicola *stops.*

Jake You're my daughter. He's your son. He hasn't heard from you for six years. It reeks of beer out here.

Nicola What else? There was always something else on your list of things, Jake.

Jake I wanted to ask you if you've got any guilt whatsoever.

Nicola Actually, you just have asked me.

Jake *walks away. He stops.*

Jake Roy, come on.

Roy *is playing with the Tamogochi, frantically.*

Roy I'm stopping here.

Nicola *eats another segment of her orange and sucks the flesh off the skin. She puts the peel into her pocket.*
Jake *comes back to the table.*
Roy *taps his knuckles on his grandfather's forehead.*

Knock knock.

He goes back to tending the Tamogochi.
Jake *looks from* **Roy** *to* **Nicola**.

Jake You call me Dad from now on. Not Jake.

Nicola *grabs hold of* **Jake**'s *ear and holds it tight.*

Nicola At this moment I completely need to see in your wallet.

Jake Let go of me.

Nicola Please. Dad.

Nicola *smiles.*
Jake *is in pain. He gets out his wallet and puts it on the table.*

Roy Let go of him, Mum.

Nicola *lets go of her father's ear. She looks at her son. She knocks the Tamogochi out of his hand and stamps on it so that it breaks. A slight pause.*
She picks up her father's wallet and rifles through it. She finds a photograph.

Nicola Is this Grandma? Is this a photograph of your mother? When did you last see her?

She looks at **Roy** *and then at* **Jake**.

I carry three photographs of him about in my bag.

Roy He last saw her when Great-granddad died.

Nicola Have you met your great-grandmother, Roy?

Roy *shakes his head.*

Roy No.

He bends down and picks up the broken pieces of Tamogochi and puts them on the table. He takes another Tamogochi from his pocket. He plays with it.
Nicola *watches him for a moment. She walks away. She stops.*

Nicola   I met Uncle William once. He was a little bit grumpy for my taste.

She comes back to the table. She takes a ten-pound note from the wallet.

I've got to get a train back to Euston.

She puts her father's wallet back in his pocket.

The answer is – yes, I do feel guilty. The actual question is – do you?

Scene Three

The Quay in Exeter. It is Monday afternoon.
Philip *is there. He has a college scarf hanging loosely from his neck. He picks up a small, flat stone, which he throws high into the air. He catches it, and then skims it across the still water of the Quay.*
Harriet *comes on. She is thirty-seven years old.*

Philip   I bet you can't guess what I'm thinking about?

Harriet   I could never guess anything about you, Philip. You're a law unto yourself, like your brother.

Philip   I'm thinking about Stonehenge.

Harriet   It was good to be there.

Philip   I'm thinking about the enormous effort involved.

Harriet   Yes.

Philip   The stone came from South Wales and it was dragged down to the sea. Then it was floated along the River Avon.

Harriet   I wish we'd stayed there longer.

Philip   Why?

Harriet   It looked very calming.

Philip   I agree.

Harriet   I do like the Quay though.

Philip   When the end comes, thousands will be at Stonehenge, looking up at the sky. It's true. And I will probably be looking up a pig's bottom.

A slight pause.

This is the first time I've been scared since I was reading in the top field and a young boar put his snout in my book. I don't want to become pork chops his eyes said to me. My heart thumped and went out to him.

She smiles at him. He pauses in his stone throwing.

Harriet   Pork chops?

Philip   That's what our family does. What do you do?

Harriet   I'm a chemist.

He throws another stone.

I read chemistry here in Exeter actually. I spend most of my time in a white coat. In the laboratory. Magnesium still gives me a thrill.

Philip   Can I ask you another question please?

She smiles at him again. He pauses in his stone throwing again.

What's going to happen?

Harriet   I don't know, Philip.

She stops smiling, briefly. He still holds the stone in his hand.

Philip   I don't think there's a single person on the whole of the earth who has the slightest idea what a cosmic string really is, do you?

Harriet   There are two strings actually.

She looks at him before she answers.

I'm a chemist, Philip. I find it all a little perplexing. I never paid much attention in Physics and I doubt you do either.

Philip *smiles.*

Thirteen billion years ago, in the fraction of a second after the big bang, when the Universe cooled down, different fields moving in different directions froze. Cosmic strings lie between those astronomical fields. Like a geographical fault line but in space rather than in California. It's started to move. It's emitting a supernova of unthinkable force at light speed. It's moving like it moved in the first thousandth of a second of the Universe.

Harriet *smiles.*

There was a time, a long time ago, when your brother liked me to wear a white coat and nothing else at all.

Philip   Well I shall look at James in an entirely different light when he comes back.

They both smile.

Will it happen, Aunt Harriet?

She looks at him again.

Harriet   I don't know, Philip. But something is happening. It really is.

Philip   Thank you.

Harriet   There's so little that we actually really know. What are you and I? What are our lives when we think of them set against thirteen billion years of history?

He skims the stone. **James** *comes on with* **Jenny**. **Jenny** *is an eight-year-old brown Labrador.*

James   You disappeared.

Philip   I left you on your own for a while.

Harriet *looks at her husband.*

Harriet   He's thoughtful and clever like that.

James *crouches down and fusses the dog.* **Philip** *picks up a small stone.*

Philip   I'll never understand why you two liked Exeter so much. Exeter is very boring. But I like swans.

He skims the stone across the water.

James   Throw it any more accurately, Philip, and you'll hit one.

James *kisses* **Jenny**'s *snout.*

Philip   You should have been the farmer.

Harriet   Do you want to know an interesting fact?

Philip   How interesting is it?

Harriet   On old galleons they used to carve a white swan on the figurehead to bring good luck. A swan never goes completely under water. Imagine a tea clipper moored here.

A slight pause.

Do you know what I'd like to do? Have a cream tea. I want to get us all a proper cream tea.

James   You'll never find a place open.

Harriet   I want us to sit here for a bit and eat some warm scones, with clotted cream, and jam, and drink three pots of earl grey tea.

James   All the cafes are closed.

Harriet   I can find one open. I'm good at that.

James   The scones will be cold.

He stops petting **Jenny** *and gets up.*

We're meant to be together. Why are you always wandering off?

Harriet   What do you think, Philip?

Philip   I have complete faith in you, Harriet. I think James is being something of a curmudgeon, and I'd like a plain scone please.

James   If you find somewhere open, get some water in a bowl for Jenny.

Harriet   She's fine.

James   She's not, she's thirsty.

Harriet *looks at* **Philip**.

Harriet   What's the longest word you know?

Philip *whispers in* **Harriet**'s *ear*.

And what does that mean?

Philip   It means the incredible feeling of having a wee in the quarry on the farm in the nude.

Harriet   You're a wonder, Philip, you really are.

She starts to go.

And you're altogether right about your brother. Wait here. I'll be back.

She goes. As she leaves she does a little skip. The two brothers watch her, and then they look at the river. **James** *strokes* **Jenny**.

Philip   We've not found Edward, have we.

James   No.

Philip   When you were at university did you drink lots and get off with lots of girls?

James   That would be telling.

Philip   More than just Harriet?

James   I certainly don't want you to tell her.

Philip   I bet your willy moved all the time.

A slight pause.

Do you think I'm fat?

James *takes out a cigarette and lights it with a match.*

James   Far too many apple crumbles.

James *smokes.*
Philip *watches him.*

Would you like to keep my scarf?

Philip   Yes, please. Look.

He lifts up his head.

One chin.

He puts his head down

Three chins.

He wraps the scarf round his neck.
A pause.

James   This is where I used to come. To go out – to the student nights.

James *smokes.*
Philip *watches him.*

Philip   Can I have one?

James   No.

Philip   Why not?

James   Because you'll get cancer and die, that's why.

A pause.

Philip   Do you wish you had never married Aunt Harriet?

James *strokes* **Jenny**.

James   What a question to ask.

Philip   Sometimes you communicate silently. I've seen on the news that quite a lot of people have regrets in middle age.

James   I'm not middle-aged.

James *stubs out his cigarette.*

Don't you go and say anything.

He takes out a packet of mints from his pocket. He sucks one.

Philip   I've not tried a cigarette yet, and I've not got off with anyone yet, but I've had three wet dreams and they wake me up with a nice feeling in my willy.

James *smiles.*

You've got an aura. Everybody has. Harriet's aura is very strong. Interestingly, she's my favourite relative.

James *laughs.*

James   The stuff you come out with. It would all go in a very long book.

James *wanders away to explore the water's edge.*
A slight pause.
Philip *wanders in the other direction. He looks at the water in the Quay.*
A pause.
Philip *takes a packet of ten cigarettes from his pocket. He removes the cellophane wrapping. He takes a cigarette and lights it with a lighter. He smokes for the first time.*
James *eventually sees him.* **Philip** *holds out his hand with the cigarette.* **James** *goes to him. He takes the cigarette from* **Philip**.

You've got it all wet.

James *smokes.*

Philip   What's going to happen in two weeks' and five days' time?

James Your guess is as good as mine. The world is crumbling, Philip.

James *smiles.*

Philip Am I too fat to have sex?

James *smiles.*

She's a long time.

A slight pause.

What did you think about that day with William?

James I hated every moment of it.

James *gives the cigarette to* **Philip**.
Philip *smokes.*

When I was at the university here, Edward ran away from the farm to come and see me. William didn't tell you the whole story. Mum didn't like Edward very much.

A pause.

He was nine. He arrived one day before I went to a lecture. I saw him hanging around when I was going back to my room in halls after breakfast. He was shivering like a wet rat, so I got him undressed, and showered, and dry, and the girls on my corridor made a tremendous fuss of him, which he adored. He was in need of a bit of fussing. I bunked off my lectures and we came down here to the Quay for the day. We just sat in the sunshine looking at the swans and ducks. Do you remember him? Do you remember Edward?

Philip *shakes his head.*

Philip No.

He tries to smoke.

Have I ever met him?

James I don't know.

A slight pause.

Philip   I hope sex is more exciting than smoking a cigarette.

He stubs it out.
James *finds the mints.*

James   Would you like a peppermint?

James *puts a mint in his mouth and gives one to* **Philip**.
They suck their sweets.
James *crouches down and fusses* **Jenny**. *He kisses her on the snout. He looks at the river.*

James   The river runs that way towards the English Channel at Exmouth, and that way to Tiverton and then up on to Exmoor.

He looks at **Philip**.

We can go to Dawlish Warren if you like. It's a nature reserve. We can see all sorts. Herons. Oystercatchers. Brent geese. Grey plover.

Philip *crouches down.*

Philip   This is hopeless. There are one hundred and twenty thousand people in Exeter. It's very spread out and we haven't a clue where he is. It's obvious that you only wanted to come down here so that you could see it again before you die.

James   Is that on page twenty-two of your very long book?

Philip *laughs.*

Philip   On page thirty-one, as a matter of fact.

A pause.

Aren't you really, really frightened?

James   No

A pause.

Jenny's keeping me going. Walking her I mean.

He pats the dog's head. He looks at his young brother.

You should come and live with Harriet and me in
Twickenham. I absolutely want you to.

Philip   You're a quandary, James. First you're this and
then you're that.

A pause.

No. I'd better not.

Harriet *returns with a large tray. On it are three tea pots, three jars
of milk, a jug of hot water, cups and saucers, three scones, jam and
cream, cutlery and napkins.*

Harriet   I told you I'd be two minutes.

James *gets up.*

James   You've been ages and ages. Where have you been
and what have you been doing?

Harriet   The cafe with the closed sign was in fact open.

Philip *gets up.*
Harriet *puts the tray on the ground.*

There was no one in. I was very quick.

Philip *looks at his watch.*

Philip   You've been gone an hour and a half.

Harriet   I was five minutes, Philip. Five minutes at most.

Harriet *organises the cream tea.*

There's something so wonderfully English about this, isn't
there?

James *looks at his watch.*

James   Both our watches can't be wrong.

Harriet   Well, I'm here now. Sit down then, you two, let's
enjoy our cream tea.

Philip *and* **James** *sit down.*

James *puts his hands above the scones.*

James   The scones are warm.

Harriet   Exactly.

Philip *looks on, enviously.*

Aren't you having any, Philip?

Philip   I might have a very small piece.

They eat the cream tea.

James   You did not get a bowl of water for Jenny.

Harriet   Yes, I'm sorry about that.

Harriet *looks at them.*
James *gives* **Jenny** *a piece of scone.*

Am I missing out on something?

Pause.
They don't answer.
James *smiles at* **Philip** *and then looks away from him.*

James   You'll never know, Philip, what it really means to miss out on something that you want very much.

Scene Four

At Mill Farm there is a tin bath. It is lit by a shaft of sunlight coming in through a skylight.
It is Wednesday morning.
Margaret *comes in. She is seventy-one years old. She rolls up her sleeve, and then tests the temperature of the water in the bath with her elbow.*
Philip *comes in. He has bucket of hot water.*

Margaret   A little more if you please, Philip.

Philip *pours some hot water into the bath.*
Margaret *stirs the water with her hand to even out the hot and cold.*

A little more.

She goes out.

Philip *pours some hot water into the bath.*
Margaret *comes back. She has a freshly laundered white towel and a bar of soap.*

Take these if you please, Philip.

Philip *puts down the bucket. He takes the towel and soap.*

Philip   Strange things have started happening.

Margaret *tests the temperature of the water with her elbow.*

It only took an hour for me to get back on the train. My watch said it didn't but my stop watch said it did.

Margaret *rolls up her other sleeve.*

One minute I was in Exeter, then next Birmingham, and then I was back here. It was quite exciting travelling on the train by myself. I thought people would be unnerved by me but they weren't.

Margaret *takes a plastic apron from between the fold in the towel that* **Philip** *is holding.*

I don't understand why James liked Exeter University so much. I think Exeter is a provincial backwater. There are too many posh boys in ripped jeans on mobile phones. Them or scrumpy men and turnip heads. The cathedral was packed with people who were praying.

Margaret *puts on the apron.*

I'd go to the University of Life. I'd go to France and hitch lifts along the motorways, and read French novels in smoky cafes.

Margaret *goes out.*
Philip *is still.*
A pause.
Margaret *comes back with* **William**.

William *is wearing a white bathrobe. His watch is on his wrist.*
Margaret *helps* **William** *to walk very slowly towards the bath.*

Can I help you with him, Mum?

They stop.

Margaret *takes hold of* **William**'s *wrist. She undoes the leather strap and takes off the watch. She puts it carefully in a pocket in the apron.*
Margaret *helps* **William** *to step slowly into the bath.*
William *grimaces. It is an effort. He is in pain.*

William   Do you think I will see the end, Mother?

Margaret   I hope so. If the end comes.

William *is still.*
Philip *puts the towel on the floor. He goes away to the corner, where there are some small, kitchen stepladders, with a metal jug on the top step. He brings them back to the bath. He picks up the towel.*
Margaret *fills the jug with warm water. She climbs the two steps. She slowly pours the water over* **William**, *wetting his hair. The water trickles down on to the bathrobe.*
Margaret *gives the jug to* **Philip** *when it is empty.*
Margaret *takes a bottle of shampoo from a pocket in the apron. She pours some on to her hand. She gives the bottle and the top to* **Philip**. **Philip** *screws the top back on and puts the bottle on the floor.*
Margaret *slowly, carefully, washes* **William**'s *hair.*
Tiny streams of shampoo trickle down on to the bathrobe, which is still fastened.
Philip *picks up the jug. He fills it with warm water. He gives it to his mother.*
Margaret *slowly pours the water over* **William**'s *head, rinsing away the shampoo. She gives the jug to* **Philip**. **Philip** *fills it. He gives the jug to his mother.*
Margaret *slowly pours the water over* **William**'s *head.*
She comes down off the stepladder. She puts the jug on the floor. She looks at her oldest son for a moment.

William   My journals are in the bottom two drawers of the grey filing cabinet in my study. You should read them.

William *catches his breath. He winces.*

Margaret   Are you in pain?

William   Yes.

Margaret *turns to her youngest son.*

Margaret   Go and fetch William's flask.

Philip *runs out.*
Margaret *looks at* **William**.

I walked five miles to slap the face of the boy who teased you at school.

A slight pause.

I put a clean shirt and pants on the bottom of your bed every Monday morning.

A slight pause.

I smacked you on the leg when you soiled your trousers.

A slight pause.

We didn't have the money you wanted. We had this farm, which I think was riches. We had the ponies for you to ride across the fields, which were yours. We even had the top field where you could look out over the sea. And you had the barns to play in.

Philip *runs in. He has a flask. He stops immediately some distance from them.*

Thank you, Philip. Give it to your brother.

Philip *goes to* **William**. *He unscrews the top of the flask. He sniffs.*

Philip   It's morphine, isn't it.

William   Yes.

William *takes the flask.*

Philip   It's heroin, isn't it.

William   Yes.

William *looks at the flask.*

No. I want to be alert when I see the end of the world.

He gives the flask to Philip. Philip *screws the top back on. He gives the flask to his mother. His mother puts it in a pocket in the apron. The brothers look at their mother for a moment.*
Margaret *turns her back so that her face is hidden from them. She fights back tears.*
Philip *bends down. He takes a flannel from between the fold in the towel. He takes the soap. He undoes the knot on the front of* **William**'s *bathrobe, but he does not take it off.*
He puts the soap and the flannel in the water. He begins to wash his brother's thin body.

Philip   While I was out, I put the potatoes on and did the carrots. I've put the lettuce in the fridge. I've hoovered round the sitting-room, Mum.

Margaret   Thank you, Philip.

Philip *washes* **William**'s *chest.*

Philip   I've put your pyjamas out to dry in the paddock.

Margaret *fights back tears. She gathers strength. She turns.*

Margaret   Can you bear me to wash you, William?

William   Yes.

She goes to him. She carefully takes off the bathrobe. She puts it in a pile on the floor.
She washes her son's body, his neck, his chest, his arms, his hands, his back, his legs, and ends with his feet. She is now kneeling. She gets up. She looks at **Philip**.
Philip *gives her the towel.*
Margaret *climbs the stepladders. She dries her son's hair. She gives the towel to* **Philip**.

She comes down off the stepladders.
William *catches his breath. He winces.*
Philip *gives the towel to his mother.*
Margaret *begins to dry her oldest son.*
William *cries out.*

Philip   Careful, Mum, you'll hurt him. You're hurting him.

Margaret *stops.*

Margaret   You do it. If you're so clever.

Margaret *looks down. She is still.*
Silence.

Philip   All I said is you were hurting him.

A pause.
Margaret *dries* **William**. *She begins with his knees and goes upwards. She dries his chest, his neck, and his back.*

Margaret   Go to the paddock, Philip, and bring William's pyjamas. They'll be dry now.

Philip   Please remember for future reference that I am not the house slave. Thank you.

Philip *runs out. He runs back in. He has* **William**'s *pyjamas, which are ironed, folded neatly over his arm.*
Margaret *dries* **William**'s *face.*
William *puts his arm on his mother's shoulder for support. He steps out of the bath.*
Margaret *bends down to dry her son's feet.*
Philip *watches her.*
Margaret *gets up. She takes the watch out of the pocket in the apron. She puts it on* **William**'s *wrist.*
William *gathers strength.*

William   I've not left anything to Edward. Jake and James can have whatever they like.

William *holds out his arm.*

I want you to have this, Philip. Grandma Dorrity gave it to me. Is that all right, Mother?

Margaret   Yes, of course.

William   It came to the oldest. It should now go to the brightest.

Philip   You're not going to die, William. I won't let you.

William   It was Karl's watch originally.

Margaret   Yes.

Philip   Who's Karl, Mum?

Margaret   He was a friend of my father. He was someone my father helped.

William   Karl escaped from the Berlin ghetto with nothing save this watch, Philip. His father got as far as Cape Town, and Karl went there eventually himself so they could be together when his father died.

Philip *looks at the watch.*

Philip   Is Karl still alive, Mum?

Margaret   I doubt it.

Margaret *takes the pyjama bottoms from* **Philip**. *She bends down.* **William** *uses her shoulder for support. She puts his legs into the pyjamas. She pulls them up.*

Philip   William.

William   Yes.

Philip   Why did Grandma Dorrity wear a man's watch?

A grandfather clock, somewhere in the house, chimes seven o'clock.

Who is Roy?

Margaret   Roy is Nicola's son.

Philip   She's smashed his Tamogochi, but he's got another one. He's clever like that. I'll have to be careful of him.

A slight pause.
Margaret *takes the pyjama jacket from him.*

Margaret   I know you've never met Roy because I've never met Roy.

She goes to **William** *and helps him to put the jacket on.*

Philip   I'm frightened. I'm really frightened.

Margaret *buttons* **William**'s *pyjama jacket.*

Scene Five

Thornfield Park in Stockport.
It is Sunday morning.
The summer sunlight is filtering through a sycamore tree.
Jake *is standing.*
Roy *is standing.*
Nicola *is standing. She has her bag. She looks at the sky.*

Nicola   It's going to rain.

Jake *holds out the flat of his hand.*

Jake   Yes. It's spotting.

Nicola   That's quite nice to me. It makes me feel nostalgic. It's always raining in Stockport.

Jake   We should have brought umbrellas. The three of us could have stood here, each of us holding an umbrella. We could have sung in the rain.

Nicola *smiles.*
A pause.

Nicola   The places on the bus route have all changed, you know. They've even changed the number of the bus. The whole town's changed really, hasn't it?

Jake   It has rather.

Nicola   What have you been doing all week?

Jake   We were packing mainly. I've still got to work ten days so I was trying to get all the packing done in the few spare hours I had.

Roy *writes on his hand with an imaginary pen.*

Nicola   What's he doing?

Jake   He's writing an imaginary letter.

Roy *looks away from his mother.*

Nicola   Who is it to, Roy?

Roy   Uncle Philip.

Jake   He's writing letters to everyone.

Nicola *looks at* **Jake**.

Nicola   I don't want you think this is easy for me, being here, because it really isn't.

Jake   No, I know that.

Nicola   It upset me seeing you last week much more than I thought it would.

Jake   Of course it did. It upset us, too.

Roy *looks up at his granddad. He puts his hands in his pockets. He looks away again.*

Nicola   I've been thinking about you all week, Roy.

Roy   Have you.

Nicola   You look very handsome. That makes me rather proud. But you are a bit spotty. You need to buy some spot cream. Do you wear deodorant now?

Roy   What?

Nicola   Do you, Roy?

Roy *shuffles from foot to foot.*

Roy   You're embarrassing me.

Nicola   Have you tried shaving yet?

Roy   No.

Nicola *looks at* **Jake**.

Nicola   You should tell him about stuff like this.

A pause.
Nicola *looks about.*
A slight pause.

It's quite smart in the park, now, isn't it?

Jake   It is, rather.

Nicola   Can you do a bronco, on the swing, Roy?

Roy   Course I can.

Nicola   I bet you can.

Roy   Do you want to see me? I can move those little kids easily. You don't even need to say anything to them. You just walk up and they move away.

Nicola   It's all right. I believe you.

Nicola *smiles at her son.*

Roy   What are you smiling at?

Nicola   You. Are you going to write an imaginary letter to me?

Roy   I have done. It's in the post. Would you like an ice cream? There's a van just behind the tennis courts.

Nicola   I would please, Roy, thank you.

Roy   Great. What about you, Granddad?

Jake   I'd like a ninety-nine.

Nicola   Yes, I would, too. Can I have raspberry sauce on mine?

Roy   Of course you can.

Jake   Here.

Jake *gives* **Roy** *a five-pound note from his pocket.*

Roy   Thanks, Granddad.

Roy *runs off.*
Nicola *and* **Jake** *watch him go.*
Jake *looks at his daughter.*
Nicola *looks away from her father. She rubs her eye with her fist. She struggles to gather her breathing. She exhales very heavily, once.*

Jake   Are you all right?

Nicola   I'm a bit upset.

Jake   Yes.

A slight pause.

He writes a letter to you every day.

Nicola   Does he?

Jake   Yes. He's doing well you know, Nicola. He's working hard at school.

Nicola   That's good. That's important. Him still going on and that.

Jake   I was going to bring one of his reports with me, but he caught me with it and insisted that I put it away. I think he was just being shy.

Jake *and* **Nicola** *look at one another.*
Nicola *looks away.*

I've not been here since you gave him to me.

Nicola   Don't, Dad. Stop.

Jake   They're closing the park down after the weekend. I think it's good that they're waiting for the weekend. They'll close all the parks in the end. They'll have to close all the museums, too, and the canal towpaths. What if all this is wrong? What if nothing is going to happen at all? You really frightened me last weekend, you know? You really damaged my ear. And I was embarrassed. And, even though he was excited to see you again, you unnerved Roy a lot.

Nicola I didn't mean to do that.

Jake No.

Nicola I'm sorry.

Jake Where are you going to be?

Nicola When?

A slight pause.

I'll be in London.

A slight pause.

Jake Come with us.

Nicola What?

Jake Come with Roy and me to Mill Farm, Nicola.

A slight pause.

Nicola I don't want to see him die.

A slight pause.

Jake He doesn't admit it but he's very frightened about what's going to happen. He wants you to be there with him, Nicola. I very much want you to be there, too. We're going to get a train at the end of next week.

Nicola I thought you were going to give me some money like you said.

Jake You could stay here with us, and then come and get on the train with us. I'd buy you your ticket. I'd buy some clothes for you to last you a week.

Nicola You have no idea what this is like for me.

Jake   I have.

Nicola   I love him.

Jake   I think you owe it to him to see him die.

A pause.

Nicola   No.

Jake   Why not?

Nicola   I can't.

Jake   You can.

Nicola   I'm falling apart.

Nicola *opens her mouth and takes out a tooth.*

My teeth are falling out.

She pulls off a finger nail.

My finger nails are coming away. I've got bruises everywhere. Some of the people I spend my time with you would not even believe could exist.

A slight pause.

I'm incredibly cold now. Have you got any cigarettes?

Jake   No.

Nicola   If I don't have a cigarette soon I don't know what I'll do.

A slight pause.

He doesn't know who I am. I don't want him to know. It's better that he doesn't. I would be such a massive disappointment to him. I couldn't face it.

Jake   That's not true.

Nicola   It really, really is true.

A slight pause.

Jake *kneels down. He takes a bundle of fifty-pound notes, tied with a rubber band, from his pocket. He puts the money on the ground. From another pocket, he takes a bundle of twenty-pound notes. He puts them on the ground.*
Nicola *kneels down.* **Jake** *takes a bundle of ten-pound notes from yet another pocket, followed by a larger bundle of five-pound notes. There is a thousand pounds in all.*

Jake   We had a code. Roy told me that when he went to get the ice creams then that was when I should ask you to come to Mill Farm.

Nicola *looks at the money.*

He told me that if I don't say anything about it, then that means you've said no.

Nicola *looks at* **Jake.**

Nobody likes him is the thing. None of his friends like him. Nobody ever comes round to play. He lies. He smokes. He takes money from me. I'm too old to do this. I see you in him. He's got your eyes. I have frequently hoped to God that he wouldn't end up anything like you.

Nicola *catches her breath.*

In the end, you know, you'll regret this. The very second before we all die, all you will feel is regret.

Nicola *takes the money. She puts it in her bag.*
Roy *comes on with three ninety-nines. He gives the one with raspberry sauce to his mother. The three of them stand, eating their ice creams.*
Roy *remembers about the change from the five-pound note and gives it to his grandfather.* **Jake** *puts the change in his pocket.* **Roy** *walks away. He kicks a small stone about. He stops.*

Roy   The boy before me got his ice creams for nothing. The Ice Cream Man told the woman behind me that he was going to drive around the town giving free ice creams to total strangers. I had to pay.

Roy *looks at his mother. He gathers strength.*

He obviously didn't like me, Mum. I don't know why. I don't know what I did wrong.

A slight pause.

They're nice, aren't they? Aren't the ice creams nice?

A slight pause.

I think they are. I think they're smashing and lovely.

Scene Six

Euston Square Gardens in London.
It is Wednesday afternoon.
James *is standing reading a book. There is a holdall on the ground beside him.*
Edward *comes on in an old wheelchair. He is twenty-eight years old. He is wearing grubby football shorts and an army greatcoat, which is open. His right leg is heavily bandaged, and the bandages are dirty.*
The wheelchair has a wooden crutch ingeniously fastened to the side of it.
Edward *takes the crutch. He struggles out of the wheelchair. He stands.*

Edward   Ten pence for a cup of tea. Twenty pence for a sandwich. Fifty pee for champagne and cocaine at the end of the world.

James *looks up.*
Edward *recognises his brother.*
James *puts the book in the back pocket of his jeans. He bends down and takes a pre-packed sandwich from the holdall. He throws it the long distance to his brother.*
Edward *catches it.*

Have you got some trousers I could have?

He shivers.

I'm freezing.

James *takes a new pair of trousers from the holdall. He throws them to* **Edward**. **Edward** *catches them.*

James   I thought if I stood in the same place long enough you were bound to come by. I realised I had to let you find me.

Edward   What about some shoes?

James *takes a pair of shoes from the holdall. He throws them to* **Edward**. **Edward** *catches them. His hands are full. He shivers.*

It's getting cold, isn't it? You probably wouldn't have noticed that, but it is. Take it from me. Take it from one who knows.

The sun comes out.
James *rolls up his shirt sleeves.*
Edward *shivers.*

I'm going to allow every single impulse in my body to go unchecked. From now on if I see something I want, I'm just going to take it. If I need to say something, I'm just going to say it. If I hate someone, I'm just going to hate them. The bubbles have floated away. The sentences that hold our world together have fractured. The oxygen is thinning. The hair is eroding. The leather on our backs has started to sweat. All of these things are true.

James *looks away.*

Are you crying, James? Don't cry. Don't start crying for your brother. I hate people crying. I really do, actually.

James *rubs his eyes with his fist.*

I need the girls of Exeter to comfort me. You won't do, I'm afraid. I don't turn tricks. You're going to have to leave me alone.

James *gathers strength. He looks up.*

UNIVERSITY OF WINCHESTER
LIBRARY

James   William is dying of cancer.

Edward   Don't pity me. I hate people pitying me.

James *bends down to the holdall. He takes out a small plastic sachet of heroin. He tips the heroin on to his palm. He blows on his palm so that the drug disappears into the air.*

James   William has cancer in his colon, and now in his hip and his liver as well.

The brothers are looking at one another.

We can go into Euston and get a burger if you want.

Edward   Are you trying to kill me or what? Have you got the slightest idea what they put in those things?

Neither brother looks away.

James   William's going to die very soon.

Edward   Well – good. I do not care one tiny jot.

James   You should have a colonoscopy.

Edward *laughs.*

If the cosmologists have got it wrong, then it's important your bowel is checked.

Edward   Are you crazy?

James   Yes. A little. But it's still important to hope.

Edward   You're a magician. Have you anything else in your bag?

James *bends down. He takes out a piece of folded cardboard and opens it out. On it is written 'Tell Edward Benton to come home to Mill Farm'.*

Tell Edward Benton to come home to Mill Farm. I knew I could smell bacon.

Edward *shivers.*

I don't suppose you've got an electric blanket in there?

James   No.

Edward *is sweating. He wipes his brow with his hand.*

Edward   I don't suppose you've got some help in there?

James   You tell me.

Edward   I don't suppose you've got champagne?

James   No.

Edward   Is life in there?

James   Yes.

A slight pause.

None of us know what we've really done to you to deserve this, Edward.

Edward *is shivering and sweating.*

Edward   By the way, I should have told you. You've categorically got the wrong man. I'm not Edward. This is a case of mistaken identity. This is completely magnificent.

Scene Seven

It is Saturday.
Philip *is standing at Mill Farm. He is reading* **William**'s *journal.*
Out of the darkness **Dorrity** *appears. She is nineteen years old. She is wearing a white night dress. She is standing in front of a large enamel bowl full of water. There is a white towel on the floor nearby. In her arms, held gently to her shoulder, is a baby.*
Dorrity *adjusts the white shawl that is protecting her young child.*
A grandfather clock, somewhere in the house, chimes five o'clock.
Out of the darkness **Karl** *appears. He is sixteen years old. He is wearing threadbare clothes. He is wearing a watch.*
Dorrity *looks at her grandson.*

Dorrity   Philip, put down your brother's journal and hold your mother's hand for a moment will you please.

Philip *shakes his head a little bit. He puts the journal on the floor.*

Karl, would you be as kind as to give my daughter to her son.

Philip *takes a step or two backwards. He gathers strength. He stops.*
Karl *goes to* **Dorrity**. *He takes* **Margaret** *gently from her.*

Philip   What if I was to drop her?

Dorrity   It's not an issue because you won't. Have you tidied your room, Karl?

Karl *shakes his head. He smiles. He takes* **Margaret** *to* **Philip**.
Philip *holds his mother. He looks at her for a while.*

Philip   Hello, Mum.

He looks at **Dorrity**.

She's asleep. She's beautiful.

Karl *adjusts the shawl.*
Philip *puts his little finger in his mother's mouth.*

She sucking on my finger in her sleep.

Karl *goes to* **Dorrity**.
Philip *looks at his mother.*

Is it right to be angry, Mum? Is it right to feel pity? Is it right to want peace? Is it right to misbehave, or run away? Is it right to be scared? Is it right not to understand very much, or not to try to? Is it right to care at all? When you find out will you let me know.

Karl *and* **Dorrity** *are kneeling at the enamel bowl.* **Karl** *is washing* **Dorrity**'s *face, using just the water and the flat of his hand.*

Is it right to keep faith in a loveless marriage?

The grandfather clock chimes two o'clock.

Karl's *face meets* **Dorrity**'s *face. He takes off his watch. He presses it in to her hand.*

Dorrity   No.

Karl   Everything I have is already yours. Please.

Dorrity *puts the watch back on his wrist.*

Dorrity   I'm afraid.

Karl   So am I.

Dorrity   I love you.

They kiss full on the lips for a while. The fingers of their hands begin to take hold and intertwine. Their arms stretch out and their knuckles become white. His kissing takes on a new passion. She responds. She digs her fingernails into his back. She helps him take off his jacket. Her fingernails get a better purchase on his skin through his shirt.

Philip *looks away slightly.*
Karl's *hand goes to her neck and throat.* **Dorrity** *puts her fingers to her lips.*

Sssh.

Karl *is still. They listen.*

Karl   She's fast asleep.

Dorrity *whispers.*

Dorrity   I thought I heard him come in.

Philip   It's all right. He's at the Quaker Meeting House in Manchester.

Karl *puts his hand on her neck and pushes her downwards. He kisses her throat, her lips. He works his way on top of her, slowly. He pushes into her.*

Dorrity *cries out. In the end it is over quickly. A slight pause.*

Philip *looks at them.* **Dorrity** *whispers.*

Dorrity   Your love for me has cursed us now.

She giggles.

That's what it's done to us. The dove-like care in you has pressed the very breath of life out of me. He is a bully in comparison. Some happiness in me has gone for ever.

She giggles.

How can I love that villain of a man?

She giggles.

I dislike his kindness. I abhor his piousness. I'm repelled by his age and maturity. More than anything else, I despise his sympathy for you.

She giggles.

To be loved by him now is to be bullied by him now.

She kisses **Karl** *full on the lips.* **Karl** *responds. Without looking,* **Dorrity** *takes the watch off his wrist. She pushes him away slightly.*

You're mine. Wherever you go, you will always be mine.

She puts the watch on her arm, close to her elbow.

Karl, please be as kind as to bring me my child.

Karl *gets up.*

Philip   I think, Mum, I am indeed extremely clever. She knows it's a love she can never tell about to anyone, that's why the watch is close to her elbow. She doesn't want to take it off, but she must take it off.

Karl *puts on his jacket. He goes to* **Philip**.

She's been asleep all the while. She's good as gold.

Karl *takes* **Margaret** *from* **Philip**.
Karl *gives* **Margaret** *to her mother.*
Dorrity *looks at her daughter.*

Dorrity   I've gone and cursed us all, my sweet child.

Karl *disappears into the darkness.*

I hope I'll see you again, Philip.

Dorrity *and the baby disappear into the darkness.*
Philip *calls.*

Philip   Mum.

He calls again.

Mum.

Margaret *comes in. She has a bundle of washing in her arms.*

Margaret   I was in the paddock. It's always something –

Philip   It's nothing much.

Margaret   It's very, very hard this, Philip.

Philip   Yes, but I know all sorts of things, and I could tell you all sorts of things that would make your toes curl and your hair stand on end. Then things would be very, very, very hard indeed.

Margaret   Make yourself useful and help me with these.

Margaret *puts the washing on the ground. She picks up a white sheet.* **Philip** *takes one end and begins to help her to fold it. It is something they have done many times.*

Philip   Did you see the snowdrops have come up in the paddock?

Margaret   Yes.

Margaret *points to a button hole in her summer dress, where there is a snowdrop. They fold a blue sheet.*

Philip   How old is Grandma Dorrity in the photograph on the landing?

Margaret   I think she's about nineteen.

Philip   How old is Granddad?

Margaret   My father was a lot older than my mother, Philip.

Philip   Was he a good man?

Margaret   He was a very good man. He helped thousands of refugees in Stockport and Manchester before and during the war. Why do you ask?

Philip   I wish I'd known him, that's all.

Margaret   At his funeral there were a thousand people. He was a Quaker. And most of them were Jewish. I was a baby, Philip.

Philip   I wonder what it was like dying in the gas chambers at Birkenhau?

Margaret   There are disasters, which are visited upon mankind, Philip. And disasters mankind visits upon himself.

They fold a sheet with a pattern of flowers on it.

Philip   It's the knowing it's about to happen, that's the terrible and numb with fear thing.

Margaret   You're thinking life is fair. It isn't. It doesn't even approach fairness.

Philip   Did you know that when you were a baby?

Margaret   Of course not. Don't be a silly boy.

Margaret *picks up a red sheet.* **Philip** *is looking down.*

Are you running out of energy?

Philip *looks up.*

Philip   No, I was just bloody well thinking.

Margaret   Don't swear, please, Philip.

Philip   You swear.

Margaret   I do not.

They fold the red sheet.

Philip   James has heard you swear. He told William and me.

Margaret   Then James has more imagination than intelligence.

Philip   What a liar you are. Why don't you be brave and tell the truth for once?

Margaret   There is no truth nowadays, Philip. There's just a lot of badness. And that includes you. Truth these days is a moveable feast. Do be quiet.

Philip   I think you mean right and wrong is a moveable feast. Like James I know about history.

Margaret *puts the red sheet on top of the others. She picks them all up.*

Don't go.

Margaret   Why? I've things to be getting on with.

Philip   I was enjoying being with you.

Scene Eight

A semi-detached house in Twickenham. It is Wednesday afternoon There is a rug on the floor.
James *is pacing the room.* **Harriet** *comes in. She is holding a piece of rolled-up carpet in her outstretched hands.* **James** *becomes still. He looks at her.*

Harriet   I hit her with the claw hammer on top of her skull. She didn't make a noise, or squeal at all, just as you said.

Silence.

I knew you wouldn't be able to put her to sleep. I'm sorry. I think I'm a bit shocked. I'm going to be sick. There's a cottage pie in the oven. It's piping hot.

James   I couldn't eat a thing right now.

Silence.

Harriet   Are you packed?

James   I have no idea what to take.

Harriet   You need to pack for a week.

James   I've no idea what the weather will be like.

Silence.

Harriet   You need to pack. You need to get yourself together.

A slight pause.

Have you packed your pyjamas?

James   Yes.

Harriet   Have you packed your soap bag?

James   Yes.

Harriet   Have you got some spare contact lenses?

James   Yes, I have.

Harriet   What about the magazines in the folder under the freezer in the first shed, are you taking those?

James   What magazines?

Harriet   You know exactly what magazines, James.

James   I haven't looked at those magazines for donkey's years.

Harriet   I wish I'd had it out with you when I first found them.

James   When was that?

Harriet   But instead I'm there in the dark, feeling guilty about having my night dress on, wondering whether you're thinking about teenage girls.

A slight pause. **Harriet** *starts to go.*

James   It's what men do.

Harriet *stops. She looks at her husband.*

It's one of the things that we do.

A slight pause.

Harriet   Is this one of the things I had to do because you're so useless and cowardly? As always, I had to be the strong one.

Harriet *goes to him. She gives him the piece of rolled-up carpet.* **James** *puts the carpet on the floor. He unrolls it. He looks at* **Jenny**, *who is dead. He is unable to control one of his legs. It shakes a little. He looks at his wife. He taps his forehead with his finger.*

James   They slaughtered my pet pig with a bolt to the top of the skull, when I was four.

James *spits in* **Harriet**'s *face.* **Harriet** *is stunned.*
A slight pause.
James *wipes some of the spittle from his wife's cheek.*

I'm sorry I'm not man enough for you.

He wipes off the rest of the spittle.

I'm sorry you always do as I ask. I have no idea why.

Harriet   As I said, one of us has to be strong.

Harriet *gathers strength.*

Shall I run you a bath? Shall I make you a cup of tea?

James   Thank you.

A slight pause.

I feel like vomiting.

Harriet *goes out.*
James *bends down. He touches* **Jenny**'s *ear. His hands and legs shake. He despairs.*
Harriet *comes in. She has a cup of tea, a digestive on the side of the saucer.*

I'm still going to take her with us to Mill Farm. She can go in the back of the car.

Harriet   You didn't want to take her alive. I have no idea why – something strange in your childhood, something peculiar that you still don't want to share. Now you want to take her dead. It's rather too late for you to change your mind. James, she'll stink.

James   I don't care.

Harriet   You can't take a dead dog to Mill Farm.

James   You can. I can. I'm going to.

James *stands up. He takes the cup and saucer from* **Harriet.**

Thank you.

James *dips his biscuit in the tea. It falls on to the rug before it reaches his mouth.*

Harriet   You are messy.

James   I'm sorry.

Harriet *goes out.*
James *takes a packet of cigarettes out of his pocket and lights one with a match.*
Harriet *comes in. She has a damp cloth and a scrubbing brush. She stops.*

Harriet   What are you doing with those?

James *looks at his wife.*

James   You know when I told you that I'd given up smoking.

Harriet   Yes.

James   I was lying.

Harriet *moves her husband.*

Harriet   Out of the way, it will stain.

Harriet *kneels down and cleans the rug.*

James   You knew, didn't you?

Harriet *gets up.* **James** *flicks cigarette ash on to the rug.*

Harriet James, this rug was from Seville.

James I've decided not to take it.

Harriet *drops the cloth and scrubbing brush. They clatter to the floor. She runs her hands through her hair.*

Harriet Can't you at least take that thing out of the back door. No, you'll go through the kitchen. Go out of the front door.

James I'm afraid I'm not going to.

James *bends down. He stubs his cigarette out on the rug. He immediately lights another one.*

I like to buy ten cigarettes, if I haven't got any, and some mints. I like to be private and smoke a couple of fags. I eat mints all the way home, by the Thames, with Jenny on the lead, and then I brush my teeth, and I shower. Sometimes I forget I've even smoked at all. Quite seriously, I've needed them to survive a life of complete catalogue-filled misery with you, Harriet darling.

He looks at his wife.

I'm sorry.

Harriet That's the third time you've said sorry in as many minutes.

James I'm nervous about seeing Jake again. I catastrophically failed with Edward.

Harriet You complain about Philip sometimes but you're really the youngest.

James Smoking is just another failure in a long list of failures. I'm sorry.

Harriet *runs her hand through her hair.*

Harriet I don't know where I am, James. I'm trying to do my best.

She looks at **Jenny**.

There are some things that I didn't want to do, but I did them for you. You promised me we would never move again. I'm very happy here. James, I don't want to die on a pig farm in the north of England. I need you to do your best, too. You're smoking right in front of me, and you're putting cigarettes out on the rug. This isn't my James. This isn't James on a Sunday.

James *takes the matchbox from his pocket. He tips the matches on to his palm. He stubs out the cigarette in the matchbox. He puts the box in his pocket. He puts the matches in his pocket.*

James   I only ever lied because I wanted you to never stop loving me.

His leg shakes. He looks at **Jenny**.

I asked you to kill Jenny because she is a dog. I want to give my time to my family, and to you, not a dog. I want to do the right thing. I find love difficult. That is why I enjoy a fag now and again.

A slight pause.

I smoked on the farm when I used to go walking on my own, picking cowslips.

A slight pause.

I used to look at my mother and wonder why she found it difficult to touch me.

A slight pause.

I have wondered if that's why I find it difficult to touch you, on occasions. I have some girly mags under the freezer in the first shed. Does it matter at all?

A slight pause.

Harriet   Your mother has things to answer for.

James   She has nothing to answer for. She's my mother.

A pause.

Harriet   I want to clean up a bit before we go, which is foolish.

James   It isn't.

Harriet   I can pack the car. I can drive, I don't mind.

A slight pause.

James   I hate the very idea of being without you.

He looks about the empty room.

We're never coming back.

Harriet   No.

James   I don't know if I can do this.

James *gathers strength.*

I'd like most to meet Benjamin Disraeli.

He smiles.

What would you like most?

Harriet   I'd like it most if you were to try to be kind.

James   What would you most like second?

Harriet   You know when I get jumpy?

She looks at him, seductively.

Jumpy, jumpy.

She stops being playful.

No, that's not what I mean.

James   What do you mean, Harriet?

A slight pause.

Harriet   I'll be in the kitchen when you're calm and we can carry on packing up.

James   Say it.

Harriet   You know the things you say to me when I get jumpy – properly jumpy, about cooking and cleaning. Just please remember those things. Remember, I have done my best. I'm just a person, that's the one thing. I'm flawed, that's the other thing.

Harriet *goes out.* **James** *is left alone.*

Interval.

Scene Nine

The end of a carriage on a train. It is Friday afternoon.
Roy *is by the door. He is looking out of the window at the countryside as it goes by. At his feet is a pile of Jaffa Cakes.*
Jake *is sitting on a case. There is another bag beside it.*

Roy   I could go and look for some seats again, if you want.

Jake   I'm all right, Roy. Thank you.

Roy *looks out of the window for a moment.*

Roy   Is it normally as busy as this?

Jake   Not normally, no.

A slight pause.

Roy   There are people in there crying their eyes out. Half of them are really old. Is this like a busman's holiday for you?

Jake   Roy.

Roy   Did you know the man with the refreshments trolley?

Jake   I didn't, no.

Roy   Don't you all know each other on the trains?

Jake   Of course we don't.

Roy *smiles. He opens one of the small packets of Jaffa Cakes and starts to eat.*

Roy Would you like one?

Jake No, thank you.

Jake *stands up. He steadies himself against the side of the carriage.*
Roy *finishes the packet of biscuits.*

Roy Were they angry about you leaving early?

Jake No, they said people can stop working whenever they
want.

Roy That's nice of them.

A slight pause.

There were twelve people in my class yesterday. I thought
that was amazing.

Roy *grins.*

When I get to Mill Farm, I've decided, I'm going to become
a robber. I'm going to go robbing. I'm going to walk around
all the cottages in the countryside, and knock on people's
doors, and if they're not in I'm going to steal their toasters
and sell their kettles. I'll make a fortune.

Jake Toasters and kettles?

Roy People love toasters. You can do anything now.

Jake *stoops to look out of the window.*

Why have you never owned a car?

Jake I could never afford one. I nearly died in one.

Roy Is that why you went to work on the trains?

Jake I've never thought of it like that.

They look out of the window for a moment.

Roy I'm very excited about going to the countryside.

Jake That's good.

Roy Will there be a lot of pigs?

Jake I think there should be.

Roy   A million or so?

Jake   I don't think there'll be a million.

Roy   Will I be able to drive a tractor?

Jake   I don't know, Roy. I don't see why not.

Roy *looks at* **Jake**.

Roy   I hope we get there before your brother dies.

Jake   Thank you, Roy.

Roy   I'd very much like to meet Uncle William. What time do we get to York?

Jake   Soon, I hope.

Roy   And what time is the connection to Middlesbrough?

Jake   Soon, after that.

Roy   What happens if we miss it?

Jake   We can't miss it. It's the very last train.

Roy   We won't miss it, take it from me, take it from one who knows.

Jake *smiles*.

What is Philip like?

Jake   He's a quiet boy. I've not seen him for a long time. Now – I don't know.

Roy   I'm going to call him Uncle Philip.

Jake   Don't you go upsetting anyone.

Roy   Do I ever?

Jake *smiles*.

Jake   No.

Roy   What's your mum like? I bet she swears like a trooper when she's out amongst the piggies.

Jake   She doesn't. You'd better not go swearing at her, Roy.

Roy   Would I ever?

Jake   No.

Roy   Why don't you like her?

Jake   I do like her.

Roy   Not quite you don't. You nearly do.

A slight pause.

Take it from someone who knows. I know about mothers.
Nothing gets past me, Granddad.

Jake   Yes, I can see it in you, Roy.

Roy   I wish I'd had a brother.

Jake's *mobile phone rings. They listen to the sound. It rings off.*
A slight pause.

Mum's going walking tomorrow, she's decided.

Jake *looks at the phone.*

She's going on her own. She told me that she's going to walk
the Pennine Way. She said she's going to try to spend the
night on Kinder Scout. She told me that was the highest point
in England. Is that true? Is Kinder Scout the highest point in
England?

Jake's *phone rings again. They listen to the sound. The phone rings
off.*
A slight pause.
The phone beeps to indicate a text message.
Jake *ignores it.*

That was a message. How many messages are there?

Jake   Roy.

Roy   How many?

Jake *looks at* **Roy**. *He looks at the phone. He looks out of the window.*

Jake   Thirty-four.

A slight pause.

Roy   She told me that if I wanted to spend the day with her then she'd like that. She told me that I was the only person that she'd like to spend tomorrow night with, at the end of the world. She said she'd buy a tent.

A slight pause.

I'm just telling you what she told me.

A slight pause.

Do you know what I told her?

Jake   No.

Roy   I told her that I was going to Mill Farm, with you. I told her I wanted to spend my last day on earth with Uncle William, even though I've never met him.

Jake   Did you?

Roy   Yes, I did. I told her I wanted to meet a proper and good mother for the first time in my life, my great-grandma.

Jake   Your mother has done her best. She's always done her best.

Roy   No.

Jake   She has, Roy.

Roy   She hasn't always done her best. She has been useless.

Jake   I won't have you say that.

Roy   You're a bit late.

A slight pause.

I told her I don't believe a word she has ever told me.

Jake   She doesn't tell lies, Roy.

Roy She does.

Jake You're not being fair.

Roy I'm being very fair.

Jake I think she was a good mother to you at times.

Roy No. She is completely incapable of telling the truth.

Jake *smacks* **Roy** *once, hard across the face.*
Roy *flinches slightly, but does not move.*

Jake You are talking about my daughter.

Roy Don't you ever hit me again. Is that clear?

Jake Yes.

Silence.

Roy The strange thing is – you are capable of seeing the truth, you just never do. Why? Are you frightened?

Jake Yes. Perhaps.

Roy Have you always been frightened?

Jake Yes.

Roy What of?

Jake Closeness. Somehow closeness. I can't explain it more than that.

Roy You were close to me.

Jake Yes, I really tried.

Roy I know.

Jake I wasn't always good.

Roy I know. But you tried.

Jake Yes. I had to make amends, you see. I had to try with you in a better way than I failed with your mother. It's not her fault.

UNIVERSITY OF WINCHESTER
LIBRARY

Roy   Yes, it is her fault.

Jake   She's a person, Roy. She thinks. She still feels pain.

Roy   Yes. She does.

A pause.

Jake   You've grown up. I should have realised.

Roy   You know when I grew up?

Jake   No. Tell me.

Roy   When I was buying the ice creams the other day. I came back and you were silent. It was extraordinary. I suddenly found some courage.

Jake   Have you got courage now?

Roy   Of course. Inside I'm shaking like a leaf. It's difficult to be close like this. It's difficult to be honest. It's much easier to say I want to go robbing.

Jake *smiles.*

Jake   I didn't do everything wrong, did I?

Roy   No.

Roy *taps his fingers on his granddad's forehead.*

Knock knock.

Jake *gathers strength.*

Jake   I've not been home since Dad died. Dad died of colon cancer. I wasn't very good with him at the end. I should have done more. I was late by a few minutes. When I got there he was dead. I want to do better with William if I can.

Roy   It's another of hell's circles, Granddad.

Jake   What does that mean?

Roy   It means everything goes in circles.

Jake *smiles.*

Jake   William tried to kill me once. He drove his car into a ditch. He was driving very fast. I was unconscious for three days. That's when they put the metal plate in my forehead. Nobody knows this, but he did it on purpose. I've never said that out loud to anybody before. No one said anything to him. My dad never did. My mum never did. And William never did.

Jake *catches his breath.*

I've not seen James or Philip or Mum or William for years.

Roy   It's another of heaven's reasons, Granddad.

Jake   What does that mean?

Roy   It means there's a reason for absolutely everything.

Jake *catches his breath.*

Jake   I don't want to go home, Roy.

Roy   Why?

Jake   I'm scared.

Roy   What of?

Jake   Mum. I'm frightened I won't live up to what she expects.

Roy   Leave her to me. Close your eyes.

Jake *closes his eyes.*

What do you see?

Jake   Nothing.

Roy   That's your sadness, Granddad.

Jake *opens his eyes.*

Jake   What do you see?

Roy   Why does Uncle Philip think he's fat?

Jake   I don't know.

Roy   He needs to be humbled, that boy.

Jake *smiles.*

Jake   You've not answered my question.

Roy   I don't see much. Why are the bed sheets red and blue at Mill Farm?

Jake   You've got me there, Roy.

Roy   I see your mother very clearly.

Jake   I thought you didn't see much?

Roy   I was lying.

Roy *picks up a packet of Jaffa Cakes. He eats one.*

I've just this last minute had another of those amazing experiences, like when I came back with the ice creams. It must be the end of the world that's doing it.

Jake   What?

Roy   Great-grandma Margaret cares about Philip. It's just she's straightforward and very honest.

Jake   What about me?

Roy   Less about you. But you care less about her than you do about me. It's a circle.

Jake   What about William?

Roy   She's trying really, really hard with Uncle William. She knows it's the end. She wants to try hard.

Jake *smiles.*

We are going to die tomorrow night. It definitely is the end of the universe.

Scene Ten

A top-floor flat on Camden High Street in London. It is Friday afternoon.
Nicola *is standing. She has four plasters on the ends of four fingers.*
Edward *is there. He is wearing the trousers and shoes that his brother gave him. He walks and looks about the room. He limps.*

Edward   Is this your place?

Nicola   Yes.

Edward   Good place on Camden High Street. A taxi office below – it must be very handy.

Nicola *takes off one of the plasters.*

What are you doing there?

Nicola   My nails are regrowing.

Nicola *holds out the top of her hand to show her fingers. She turns her hand over. In her palm is plastic bag full of cannabis.* **Edward** *takes it.*

Edward   Let me pay you.

Nicola   No.

Edward *delves into his pocket and brings out a bundle of ten-pound notes.*

Edward   Let me pay you, please.

Nicola   Money is not worth anything any more.

Edward   You can't let me have an ounce of weed for free. Not in London. Even at this unusual moment in the history of mankind I would feel like a monumental scrounger.

Nicola   You've got a very elaborate vocabulary for a homeless ponce.

Edward   I come from quite a posh family.

Nicola   Tell me about it. I know that story.

Edward You've got a very elaborate streak of elegance for a brass-cum-dealer. I don't know what I can do for you. I would offer you my penis.

Nicola *pulls a face and then smiles at him.*

Nicola Can I ask you something?

Edward Of course you can.

Nicola What are you doing tomorrow night?

Edward *pulls a face and then smiles at her.*

Edward I've not decided.

Nicola I'm going on a train journey.

Edward Are you?

Nicola Definitely.

Edward I thought the trains are stopping running.

Nicola They'll run a train for me.

Edward Where are you going to go on your own train?

Nicola There are these chimney stacks just north of Leicester. They're these huge concrete funnels that burrow into the centre of the earth. I'm going to go and look at them. There's the Angel of the North south of Newcastle. I'm going to go there, too. I'm going to go to Theatre of Dreams which is the nickname of Old Trafford, the home of Manchester United Football Club. There's the Bullring in Birmingham. The Forest of Dean. Kinder Scout at the heart of the Pennine Way. Carlisle train station. Blackpool Tower. The monoliths at Stonehenge. The Thames Estuary has a boat nestled on its bed, at its mouth, which is so packed full of unexploded Second World War bombs that it would destroy the mouths of Kent and Essex. I thought I'd go and have a look at that as well.

Edward *paces the room for a moment. He limps. He stops. He looks at her.*

I had an altercation with a man defecating on the perfume counter in Selfridges. There was a dead policeman at his feet, and Chinese food all over the floor. He told me he had killed a traffic warden as well. He said the traffic warden was putting tickets on all the cars parked on Bond Street. The man on the counter said it was mint. I put a bread knife through him. I have always wanted to kill. But it was very banal and completely dull. He fell. I walked away.

A pause.

Edward   I know wherever I am I'll be wasted. I have a feeling there'll be one unlucky person left alive, in Ethiopia.

Nicola *looks at him.*

Nicola   What's your name?

Edward   You know my name.

Nicola   What's your real name?

Edward *thinks.*

Edward   It's Edward.

Nicola   Well, Edward, old chum, I have to tell you that if you spend your last few hours mashed on weed you'd regret it for the rest of your life.

Edward *laughs.*

Edward   I don't believe in life after death so I won't be reflecting upon it later. What's your real name?

Nicola   Angela.

Edward   You don't look like an Angela.

Nicola   What do Angelas look like?

Edward   Blonde.

Nicola *laughs.*

You could stay with me tomorrow night. If you wanted to that is.

Nicola   You don't even know me.

Edward   I've scored off you for six months. Of course I know you.

Nicola   Haven't you got a family?

Edward   No.

Nicola   Me neither.

Edward   Angela. You're a hopeless liar.

He looks at her. He thinks.

Don't be on your own. As you're counting down the seconds share the moment in a shop window full of televisions, watch the noble sort who volunteers to commentate on the end of the world for the BBC. But if you're capable of it, even a tiny bit, make sure you're with someone.

Silence.

I have nothing more to say to you.

Nicola   It's your little acts of kindness that make you good to know, Edward.

Silence.

Edward   I'll see you later, Angela.

Nicola   I'll see you later, Edward. Good luck.

Edward   Yes. Good luck to you, too.

He starts to go.

Nicola   You're the only man who has said please or thank you to me in my entire life.

Edward *stops. He looks at her.*

Edward   I don't believe that for a second.

Edward *goes.*

A slight pause.
Nicola *removes a plaster from the end of one of her fingers.*

Scene Eleven

A field at Mill Farm. It is Friday afternoon.
Philip *is by an electric fence. He is wearing his school uniform. He has a long blade of grass. He touches the fence with the end of it. His hand jumps and a tingle goes up his arm.* **William** *appears. He appears to be fit and healthy. He is wearing pyjamas.* **Philip** *senses his brother is there and turns to him, slowly.*

William   I used to do that. When I was your age, I used to do exactly the same thing. Lick your finger.

Philip *licks the end his finger.*
A slight pause.
Philip *touches the fence with his finger. He gets a bigger shock. He shakes his hand a couple of times.*

You're not a farmer, Philip. You'll never be a farmer.

Philip *stands up. He gathers strength.*

Philip   What do you want?

William   I've come to say goodbye.

Philip   People are getting better all over the place.

William   They're getting better from things they can do something about. I can do nothing about my cancer.

A slight pause.
William *sits down. He stretches out his legs. He leans back on his hands to let his face take in the summer sun.*
A slight pause.
Philip *sits down near his brother.*

I'd give you more than a penny for them.

Philip   What?

William   Your thoughts are priceless.

Philip   Why did Edward run away to Exeter?

William   I think he was lonely.

Philip   Yes, you can be lonely when you're nine. What happened when he got back, William?

William *looks at his brother.*

William   When he was eleven he packed a bag, with clothes and toys, and came to live with me in a cottage on the farm. I wasn't expecting him. He was just on my doorstep early one morning. He was my responsibility. I think I was a very poor substitute father to Edward. I know it is evil to have a brother in your life and to show him no love because there is no love in yourself.

Philip *thinks.*

Philip   Are you gay?

William   What do you think?

Philip   I don't think you are. It's somewhere in the family though. It's somewhere in our history. You know Grandma Dorrity.

William   Yes.

Philip   Did she love Granddad?

William   If you're asking me the question, you must know the answer. She didn't.

Philip   I know. She loved Karl.

William *picks up a blade of grass. He puts it in his mouth and chews the end of it.*

Don't look at me.

William   Why?

Philip   I don't know. Don't look at me.

William   What are you guilty about, little brother?

Philip *looks away.*

You've been remarkable with Mum, Philip. She cares deeply about you.

Philip   Are you envious?

William   Yes.

Philip *gathers strength. He looks at* **William**.

Philip   I don't know precisely when you're going to die.

William   In a very short while. We can still talk.

William *takes the blade of grass out of his mouth. He leans back on his hands and looks at the sun.*

It's hot today.

Philip *takes off his school blazer.*

I'll give you a thousand pounds for them.

Philip *puts his blazer neatly on the grass.*

Philip   You've made amends for Edward.

William   Yes, I've tried to.

Philip   Like Mum has tried as well.

William   Like Mum.

Philip   I'm the lucky brother.

A slight pause.
William *sits up.*

William   Goodbye, Philip.

He takes the watch off his arm. A church bell begins to toll in the distance. **Philip** *gathers strength. He leans forward and picks up the watch from where it is sitting on* **William**'s *leg. He undoes his shirt sleeve. He starts to put the watch on his wrist.*

If you look on the back you'll see it's engraved.

Philip *looks.*

Philip   Karl.

William   Karl Steiner.

Philip   It's amazing how love can destroy a life, as well as make a life fulfilled.

He puts the watch on his wrist.

Why did she give it you?

William   I was the oldest.

Philip   It's got to be more than that, something this important, especially in this family.

William   I think I reminded her of Karl in some small way.

Philip   You mean you're circumcised, William.

William *smiles.*

I've seen your willy and its intactness is fairly alarming. It's never been up a girl's whatsit. Mine's never been up a boy's whatsit, which is a shame. We're not two peas in a pod, we're two virgins in a meadow.

Philip *picks up a blade of grass and runs it between his fingers.*

I've gone and cut myself now, like a paper cut.

He wipes away a small trace of blood.

William   It'll mend.

Philip   It's always hardest being the oldest in a family because you take all the flak, and suffer the psychology of it all.

William *leans back on his hands and looks at the sun.*

William   Your philosophy knows no limits.

Philip *looks away from his brother. He lies flat on the grass with his hand on his elbow. A single tear rolls out of his eye and on to his cheek.*

William *sits up.*

Philip   We're no good at touching in this family, kissing and that sort of malarkey. Goodness knows what Mum's doing now.

William   She's with me. She's touching my cheek. She's got a small mirror which she's holding to my lips. She's looking to see if there is any mist. She's closing my eyes with the touch of her fingers, and as she does so

Philip   she feels so alone like her world has ended too early. I know.

Philip *sits up. He looks at his watch.*

William   Karl was given the watch by his father at his bar mitzvah. Karl's father had made it. He was a jeweller in Berlin. Didn't Dorrity tell you?

Philip   I've only met her once, and she was rather too preoccupied with her amorous boyfriend to think too much about me.

William *picks up a blade of grass. He chews the end of it.*

William   She once swore me to secrecy.

Philip   I even prefer secrecy to chocolate.

William   Dorrity had a little purse where she kept her cigarettes. Mum doesn't know this. You know what Mum's like about smoking. Dorrity isn't who Mum thinks she is. She took my arm one day – I would be almost exactly your age, Philip – and we walked across these fields for hours. She told me I should be in love with life. She told me I should love every girl I would ever see in as full a way as possible, and that I should light a cigarette in front of Mum to prove that I could love a girl in as full a way as possible. She had the devil's wings.

William *gets up. He goes to electric fence.* **Philip** *watches him.* **William** *licks the end of his finger. He touches the wire. He gets a shock and disappears. A single tear drops out of* **Philip***'s eye and on to the grass.*

Dorrity *appears strolling across the field. She is wearing a white dress. She has a purse, a bunch of bluebells that she has picked, and a white parasol.* **Philip** *gets up to be polite.* **Dorrity** *stops.*

Dorrity   Hello, Philip. How are you?

Philip   I'm awfully fine, thank you. Hello, Dorrity. How are you?

Dorrity   I'm very well, thank you.

A slight pause.

It's such a beautiful day.

Philip *looks away.*

Don't be shy.

She strolls towards him.

I sometimes wonder if you haven't got two personalities, the loud and the quiet. By the way, I much prefer the loud, so please do your best. Shall we sit together for a moment?

Philip *takes the parasol.* **Dorrity** *settles on the grass.* **Philip** *gives her the parasol. He sits.*
A slight pause.

You must ask me a question else I shan't know what to say.

A slight pause.

You're a sweet boy. I'm not a sweet woman. Oh, I was once, once upon a time. You saw me with Karl, and that forever must be our secret. Karl is still alive, by the way. He is in Israel, in Jerusalem. He never knew. I now speak of your grandfather, Philip. He never knew of the frank and full ways in which Karl cherished and praised me, though I sometimes think he noticed the twinkle in his eye. He brought Karl into our home. Of course it was a generous thing to do. He was a man who cared deeply about much. If someone in need asked for a shilling, then it was given. You've heard your family say there were a thousand people at his funeral, and it is true. To this day, should you go to the synagogue in Stockport, you will notice his name honoured on the wall. But like all men he had weakness. Would you have a can of something? My throat is a little dry.

Philip *goes into his blazer pocket. He finds a can of soft drink. He gives it* **Dorrity**. **Dorrity** *opens the can. She drinks a little.*

On our wedding night, your grandfather bullied me, Philip, until I was much bruised and hurt. Sadly for us all, your mother was born of that bullying. I once told William about this in this very field. I told him he should love, and love purely, but it crippled him for life. Your grandfather never did it again. As I said to your brother when he was fourteen, this will forever be our secret, and he was true to his word. My sadness is not that I loved Karl, but that in a moment of weakness I spoke to your beloved brother about these matters. I hope you will forgive me now, since that is the bravest thing to do.

The church bell stops tolling.

Scene Twelve

The main room at Mill Farm. It is Friday afternoon.
Margaret *is standing looking out of the big farmhouse window. Sunlight is slanting across her face. She has* **William**'s *crumpled pyjamas draped over her arm.*
James *comes in from the kitchen. He has an enamel bowl full of water and a white towel. He stops. He looks at his mother.*
Harriet *comes in from the hall. She has her arms full with a cauliflower, a cabbage and some carrots. She stops.*

James   William has died.

A slight pause.

Harriet   I was just getting some carrots from the barn.

She looks at them both.

I'm sorry.

A slight pause.

James   I was in the lavatory. Mum was with him on her own. It's the most complete failure of my life.

Margaret *looks at* **James**.

It seems churlish to say so now but I didn't realise my brother disliked me so intensely.

A slight pause.

He wanted us to see the end of the world together. Me, Jake, Edward and Philip. It was the most courageous thing William did in his life.

He looks at his mother.

It's what you should have wanted, Mum, but you left it to him. You should be more than a little bit ashamed.

Margaret   He was shrinking in the last days.

She gathers strength.

He was very little. His pyjamas had started to grow all over him. I stood there trying to remember what it was like when your father died. I couldn't remember anything apart from him gradually becoming quite cold. It's the one thing as a mother you are never supposed to see. Where were you when your father died?

A slight pause.

I know you weren't here. I know you've always done exactly as you wanted. Have I ever been invited to Twickenham?

She looks at **Harriet**. *She unleashes anger.*

Have I, Harriet?

A slight pause.

Harriet   No.

A slight pause.

Margaret   Many are the times I would have liked to picture you both in your home.

A slight pause.

Harriet   We thought you had William.

Margaret   William thought I had you.

A slight pause.

Harriet   We thought you were busy with Philip.

Margaret   Your thoughts were wrong.

She looks at **James**.

Why is it always my fault?

James *looks at* **Harriet**.

Harriet   It isn't.

Margaret   Why do I always feel it's my fault?

A slight pause.

Harriet   It's nobody's fault.

Margaret   Yes, it is. It's somebody's fault.

A slight pause.

Harriet   He's a useless lump at the best of times.

Margaret   There are some carrots in the kitchen.

Harriet   I couldn't find them.

A slight pause.

I don't know if teenage boys like vegetables. Does Roy like carrots?

A slight pause.

Margaret   I don't know, Harriet.

She gathers strength.

I'd like to bury William on the farm.

She looks at **James**.

I'd like you to dig a hole in a place you went as boys.

A slight pause.

James   A place I went or he went?

Margaret   You choose. I think Jake will be here soon. Have you spoken to him?

James   I've left him thirty-four messages.

Margaret   Talk to Jake as well. I'd like it to be all your places.

A slight pause.

James   There's the quarry where we took the horses, Mum.

A slight pause.

It was always a place full of hope. I think William was very human.

He gathers strength.

You have not been at fault.

Margaret   Yes, I have.

A slight pause.

Did I frighten you when you were children?

A slight pause.

James   Yes.

A slight pause.

Margaret   I know why you'd go to the quarry for the whole day. I'd rather he wasn't buried in the quarry.

James It was our place.

Margaret *gathers strength.*

Margaret The quarry it is then.

A slight pause.

Do I frighten you now?

James Yes.

A slight pause.

Margaret You were loved.

A slight pause.

James No.

A slight pause.

Margaret I did try.

A slight pause.

James It wasn't enough, I'm afraid.

Margaret Yes.

A slight pause.

James I'll take this up.

James *goes out into the hall.*

Margaret What has he said about me?

A slight pause.

Harriet I don't listen to much of it.

Margaret You should.

Harriet James is a conundrum.

Margaret Is he?

Harriet We women must stick together.

Margaret *looks at her daughter-in-law.*

No one can do enough for James. God couldn't do enough for James. It's why I love him. He's so dependent on me. He goes to pieces at the drop of a hat. It's just infuriating on occasions.

Margaret   I didn't know that.

Harriet   He's excellent at silence.

Margaret   Yes.

A slight pause.

I –

A slight pause.

Thank you.

A slight pause.

Harriet   What?

Margaret   I hit him once on the back of his leg, and he didn't speak to me for a week.

Harriet   I thump him all the time.

Harriet *puts the vegetables on the floor. She goes to* **Margaret**. *She takes hold of* **Margaret**'s *hands.*

Margaret   Is he loving, to you? Does he love you?

Harriet   Yes.

Margaret   My mother wasn't loving towards me. Can that be between us, what I've just said?

Harriet   Yes.

Margaret   I don't know why she didn't want me. I know it's hurt me all my life. Is that silly?

Harriet   No. I don't think so.

Margaret   James and I could never touch like this. There were many days when I tried to get close to my mother. It went on until she died. I'm still raw with it.

Philip *comes in from the kitchen. He sees the two women. He stops.*

Philip   I'm sorry.

He turns to go.
Roy *comes in from the hall. He stops.*
Philip *stops.*
Harriet *lets go of* **Margaret**'s *hands.*

Silence.

Roy   I'm Roy.

Philip   I'm Philip.

Roy *goes to* **Philip**.

Roy   It's very nice to meet you, Uncle Philip.

Roy *and* **Philip** *shake hands.*

How are you?

Philip   I'm very well, thank you. How are you?

Roy   I'm very well, thank you.

Roy *looks at* **Margaret**.

You must be Great-grandma Margaret.

Margaret   Yes.

Roy *goes to* **Margaret**. *He kisses her on the cheek.*

Roy   And Harriet.

Harriet   Yes.

Roy *kisses* **Harriet**'s *cheek.*
Silence.

Roy   Granddad is paying the taxi.

Philip   Did you have a good journey?

Roy   Yes, we did, thank you for asking.

Jake *comes in from the hall. He has the case and the bag.* **Roy** *goes to him. He takes the bag. He puts it down.* **Jake** *puts the case down.*
A slight pause.

Harriet   William is dead. He died a few minutes ago.

A slight pause.

Roy   I'm sorry, Granddad.

A slight pause.

Jake   We didn't make it in time.

Harriet   No.

A pause.

Jake   Where's James?

Harriet   He's upstairs.

Jake   Should I help him?

Harriet   No.

A pause.

Would either of you like something to eat?

A slight pause.

What about you, Roy? What are you like about vegetables?

Jake   Perhaps you could fry me an egg.

Silence.

Margaret   It's the incidental things you remember. When James would come back with a buttercup, or you would take your Dinky cars outside and make roads in the dust.

She looks at **Jake.**

I remember the silence in this house when you got your girlfriend pregnant, which wasn't incidental at all, because you were only seventeen.

Jake   Don't, Mum.

Margaret   I will have my say. We knew the marriage wouldn't last. I looked at the slip of a girl and knew she was an excuse for something. You were clever at school, you threw it away. Have you been happy?

A slight pause.

It's not a fair question, I suppose.

Jake *gathers strength.*

Jake   I've been happy of sorts.

Margaret   You were never one for the truth, Jake. Your life meandered along in a shambolic sort of way, when it promised so much. I remember thinking you would be the practical one. You could cook and sew and knit. If I recall correctly you knitted a sweater for James. It was a bit messy, but there was real kindness in it.

A slight pause.

Jake   Yes.

A slight pause.

Margaret   I can't even remember her name. I know she was an excuse to get away. We gave you all the money we had, to try to help you both set up a home. She took it all, didn't she, because you couldn't stop her. You couldn't stop the men who came round when you were at work. She took you for the fool that you are, Jake.

Silence.

You didn't even fight for your daughter. You just let that slip of a thing take her. At least I fought for my children. You're weak.

Silence.

Roy *looks at* **Margaret**.

Roy   You're a cunt.

Silence.

Margaret   Yes, I am. You're right.

Margaret *starts to fall over.* **Harriet** *grabs her to stop her falling.*

Harriet   Help me with her, Philip.

Philip   No.

Harriet   Help me with her, one of you.

Harriet *eventually manages to get* **Margaret** *into a sitting position without any help.*

I think she just fainted for a moment.

Harriet *picks up* **William**'s *pyjamas. She folds them and puts them in a neat pile.* **Margaret** *picks up the pyjamas and throws them across the room.*

Margaret   How dare you go and die.

Margaret *cries out. She weeps for her son.*
A pause.
Philip *goes to* **Roy**. *He takes a snail from his blazer pocket.*

Philip   I found this in one of the fields. It's a snail.

He looks at **Roy**.

Well done.

Roy   Thanks.

Philip *puts the snail in his pocket.*

Philip   You can run right round this house. It's got two staircases. It was built in sixteen hundred and four by some Carthusian monks. It's got some holes in the floorboards, so if you peal back the rugs you can look down on what's happening below.

He points his finger upwards.

Like James is doing now.

Roy *looks up, briefly, and then looks at* **Philip**.

Roy What's your snail called?

Philip Sammy.

Roy He's due a feed.

Philip He's on a diet.

Roy *goes and picks up* **William**'s *pyjamas. He gives them to* **Philip**.

Thanks.

Philip *looks at* **Jake**.

I'm Philip.

Jake It's nice to meet you, Philip.

Jake *takes* **Philip**'s *right hand in his own hands.*

You won't remember me. You were just a baby.

Philip I remember you a tiny bit. Thank you for the birthday cards.

Jake *nods.*

Jake It's been a pleasure.

Philip She doesn't mean it.

Jake I know.

Philip Thank you for coming.

Jake You're welcome, Philip.

Philip *goes to his mother. He gathers strength. He sits on the floor.*

Philip You know what, Mum? This whole family is like a colony of flabbergasted penguins.

Margaret You're in one of your silly moods.

Philip   I'm not in one of my silly moods. I'm in one of my being helpful moods.

Margaret   Yes.

A slight pause.
Margaret *starts to get up.* **Philip** *decides to help her.* **Margaret** *decides to accept his help. It is the first time they have touched each other in a long time.*
Roy *goes to help.* **Margaret** *accepts his arm.* **Margaret** *is standing.*

Thank you, Roy. I don't know where you want to sleep tonight. You can go in with Philip, or you can go wherever you want. You can go in one of the barns if you like with a sleeping bag.

Roy   A barn.

Margaret   It's only for one night.

Roy   Yes.

Margaret *slowly looks at* **Jake**.

Margaret   When did you last come home?

Jake   This isn't my home. It hasn't been my home for years.

Margaret   I know why you didn't come home.

Jake *gathers strength.*

Jake   Mum, you've got to let go of us. Like I've had to let go of Roy. It was Roy who got us here today.

Margaret   You never let go of your children completely.

Jake   You've got to stop all this.

Margaret   I hurt myself more than I ever hurt you.

A slight pause.

Jake   I'll go and find James.

Jake *goes out into the hall.*
Roy *looks at* **Margaret**.

Roy I'll go with him.

Roy *goes out into the hall.*
Philip *wanders away to the window and looks out.*
Margaret *looks at* **Harriet**.

Margaret What must you think of us? I'm sorry you had to hear all that.

A slight pause.

I know you don't like me.

Harriet That's not true.

Margaret Isn't it? I wouldn't blame you if you didn't like me.

Harriet It isn't true.

Margaret It should be true. I'm a difficult person to like.

Philip *goes out into the kitchen.*

Harriet Jake is right.

Margaret Is he?

Harriet You've got to learn to let go.

A slight pause.

Margaret It's difficult to listen to your children sometimes.

A slight pause.

It's frightening when you know your children are cleverer than you.

Harriet I won't ever know that.

Margaret I'm sorry. I'd forgotten.

A slight pause.

I want to thank you for coming. James is right – I should have been the one who brought the family together. I'm frightened about tomorrow night. I think I'm frightened of everything.

A slight pause.

This is all so exhausting.

A slight pause.

Why can't I love my children? Do you know?

Harriet *takes hold of one of* **Margaret's** *hands.*

Harriet   I think you're wrong. I think you love them too much.

Margaret   Do I?

A slight pause.

I've always thought I didn't.

A slight pause.

I did try. It was the trying that hurt so much. And the always failing. The endless doubt. I failed with Edward. That is absolutely true. There is no salvation from that, there really isn't. I broke my child's heart.

Silence.

Harriet   Yes.

Margaret   I don't know what to do to mend it. What do I do?

A slight pause.

Harriet   I don't know.

Margaret   There's nothing I can do. It's too late. It's all over.

A slight pause.

I'd give anything for a year, a month, a day. I'd give my life for that.

A slight pause.

Harriet   We must do the best we can.

Margaret   Yes.

Harriet   They're not going to do it. They're men. You must do the best you can.

Margaret   Yes.

Harriet *lets go of* **Margaret**'s *hands. She goes to the vegetables and picks them up. She goes out into the kitchen.*
Jake *comes in from the hall. He is carrying the enamel bowl full of dirty water.*

You must be exhausted, aren't you?

Jake   I'm fine.

Margaret   Would you like to stay in your room? I can get your room ready very easily.

Jake *stops.*

Jake   Mum, I don't want to be any trouble.

Margaret   It's no trouble. How could you ever be a trouble to me?

A slight pause.

I don't know what to say.

Jake   No.

Margaret   It's lovely to see you. I'm very glad you're here.

Jake *goes out into the kitchen.* **James** *comes in from the hall. He has the towel, which is soaking wet.*

This is all so very odd.

James *stops.*

James   Mum –

UNIVERSITY OF WINCHESTER
LIBRARY

Margaret   What is it, James?

James   There's no good time to say this, but I should tell you now that William is gone.

Jake *comes in from the kitchen. He stops.*

I found Edward. I saw him in London. He was in Euston Square. He's a beggar.

A slight pause.

He's fine. But he won't come up. I did try to ask him.

Margaret   I see.

James   No, you don't see. I lied to William. I told him he was coming. The very last thing I said to my brother was a lie.

A slight pause.

Margaret   He will understand.

James   Will he?

Margaret   He will respect you for it.

James   Will he?

Margaret   If he's the man I know he was. Yes, he will.

Scene Thirteen

Philip's *bedroom at Mill Farm. It is Saturday morning.*
Philip *is sitting on the edge of the bed. He is wearing boxer shorts and socks.* **Margaret** *comes in. She has* **Philip**'s *clothes.*

Philip   There's a sign on the door, Mum. You can't miss it. It's in a delicious shade of turquoise and there are three exclamation marks, which means you're supposed to knock.

Margaret *lays a white shirt on the bed.*

Margaret   James has dug a hole in the quarry.

Philip   I'm practically naked.

Margaret *puts a black tie on top of the white shirt.*

Margaret   Harriet is jugging kippers.

She unzips the case with **Philip**'s *black suit inside.*

Roy is driving a tractor.

Philip   Jake is in his counting house counting out his money.

Margaret *lays a pair of trousers on the bed.*

Margaret   I've made some apple crumbles.

Philip   Mummy, there are only so many apple crumbles you should feed a boy with a pillow tummy.

Margaret *lays a jacket on the bed.*

Margaret   Where are your shoes?

Philip   Under the bed.

Margaret   Will they walk out on their own, or are you going to find them?

Philip *bends down and takes a pair of black shoes from under the bed.*

It just remains for you to get dressed.

Margaret *sits down beside him.* **Philip** *looks at his mother in her best dress. He gathers strength.*

Philip   I'm a poof. I'm queer. I'm very gay. I think about kissing difficult boys and imagine them doing rude things to me in the paddock at dusk.

Margaret   You're in one of your helpful moods.

Philip   I am.

Margaret   Pass me a shoe.

Philip *gives her a shoe.*

Have hormones suddenly come upon you, or did you have to go and find them?

Philip   They flew in one morning through the open window.

Margaret *has some black polish and a brush.*

Margaret   Was it a morning when the world looked like a brighter place?

Philip   My private parts did things which were actually quite embarrassing considering I was on the school bus.

Margaret *polishes the shoe.* **Philip** *stands up and starts to put on the white shirt.*

I just thought you should know, Mum. There's no point in pretending any more.

Margaret *looks up at her youngest son.*

Margaret   I don't know if there'll be another moment when we're alone together.

Philip   Why do you think I've waited? We should play a game of whist – whoever wins is vicar for the day.

Margaret *smiles.*

Margaret   Quaker funerals don't have a vicar.

Philip   I can think up several lovely prayers for the midnight hour.

Margaret   On current form, I think you'd better not.

Philip *picks up the trousers. He puts them on. He gathers strength.*

Philip   Why did you have me?

Margaret *looks at her son.*

You don't have to say if you don't want to.

Margaret   No.

A slight pause.

I want to put it in a way you will understand, Philip. Your father's hormones raced up the stairs one day and quite took me by surprise.

Philip I deserve this.

Margaret Yes, you do.

A slight pause.

I didn't think you were possible. I expected the worst when I went to the doctor and he told me he could feel a hard abdominal mass in my stomach. He suspected ovarian cancer and so did I. But I had a scan and it was you, Philip. I was a day shy of my fifty-eighth birthday and there you were. What rich possibility this world is full of.

Margaret *puts the shoes on the floor.*

Margaret Try that one.

Philip *steps into it.*

Philip You've missed a bit.

Margaret It'll do.

Margaret *starts to clean the other shoe.*

Philip Thank you, Mum. It is why I asked.

Margaret I went on having boys, when I crossed my fingers for a daughter. If I'd put you in a dress you would have looked quite pretty.

Philip At midnight tonight you'll be sorry about that.

Philip *glances at his watch.*

Why did his hormones race up the stairs?

Margaret They didn't so much race up, as summersault up in a series of cartwheels and come out in a little spurty fizzle at the end. He was old by then.

Philip Mum, that's very rude.

Margaret   Is it? You're not the only person who can be vulgar, Philip.

A slight pause.

Philip   I'm tremendously shocked.

Margaret   I was never meant to be on a farm. It affected my delicate sensibility a long time ago. I've been too long with the pigs.

Margaret *looks at her son.*

What is it now?

Philip   This isn't fair, you know.

Margaret   I think it's one of the fairest things I've done in my entire life. Try this one.

She puts the shoe on the floor. **Philip** *steps into it.*

Philip   You've missed another bit.

Margaret   Come here.

Philip *moves the few inches to her.* **Margaret** *fastens* **Philip**'s *shoe laces.*

Have you washed behind your ears?

Philip   I've got an allotment of sprouts growing behind them.

Margaret   We shall eat heartily tonight then.

Margaret *stands up.*

Collar up. Button fastened.

Philip *lifts the collar of his white shirt. He fastens the top button of his shirt.* **Margaret** *picks up the black tie.*

Philip   You should have treated me like this a long time ago.

Margaret   Should I?

Philip   No.

Margaret *starts to fasten the tie. She gathers strength.*

Margaret Your father went off sex for a very long time. To this day I have no idea why, and I don't know why he was able to start again. I know I wished for the sex that we should have had. It upset me thinking about it. Edward had to go and live with William, I was so upset. When he was able to start again, you were born.

Philip *turns down the collar of his shirt.* **Margaret** *picks up the jacket. She helps* **Philip** *to put it on.*

You look like a proper man.

Scene Fourteen

A stubble field of recently cut wheat at Mill Farm. It is Saturday, early evening. There are small, dead birds all over the place. **Philip** *runs on. He is wearing his suit, but not the tie.* **Roy** *runs on. He is in his best clothes. He has a cricket bat.* **Philip** *picks up a dead bird. He throws it at* **Roy**. **Roy** *hits it back towards* **Philip** *with the bat.* **Philip** *jumps to try to head the bird, but misses.*

Philip I can't run as fast as you.

Philip *catches his breath.* **Roy** *picks up a dead bird. He looks at it, and then spreads its wings out. He opens its beak. He takes a worm out of its mouth.*

Roy This one was eating a worm when it died.

Roy *throws the bird into the air and hits it away with the bat. He looks at* **Philip**.

Use your inhaler.

Philip *takes an asthma inhaler from his pocket. He shakes it.* **Roy** *goes to him.*

It's empty. Use mine.

Roy takes an asthma inhaler from his pocket. He gives it to **Philip**. **Philip** *uses it.*

I didn't see it was empty until you took it from your pocket.

Roy walks away. He picks up a stray head of wheat.

I liked your brother's coffin.

Philip   It was rather ingenious, wasn't it? And it was actually appropriate. I think if William had known that he would be buried in wood from part of a pig hut

Roy   he would have been quietly tickled.

Roy *chuckles.*

Philip   What are you chuckling for? Have I done something wrong?

Roy   No.

Philip   Yes, that is what I was going to say.

Roy   I know. I beat you to it.

Roy *goes to* **Philip**.

Keep it. It's yours.

Philip *puts the inhaler in his pocket. The two boys look at one another.*

When we were coming back from the funeral – did you notice the Viking walking next to James?

Philip *nods.*

Philip   Yes. It was quite incredibly scary.

Roy   I knew you had. Why didn't you say?

Philip   I didn't know if you'd seen him. James definitely didn't see him. The Viking looked mightily confused, didn't he?

Roy   I wanted to say let's stop and have a chat.

Philip   Are you frightened?

Roy *nods.*

Roy   Are you?

Philip *nods. He looks at his watch.*

Philip   Six hours to go.

A slight pause.

Roy   I've never seen my granddad cry before.

Philip *nods.*

It's horrible, isn't it, watching people cry. I've only seen you cry once.

Philip *nods.*

I wanted to ask the Viking what he thought was happening.

Philip *nods.*

I'm glad you told your mother you're gay. Touch me if you want.

Philip *runs the side of his finger down the length of* **Roy**'s *cheek. The sun is setting. The shadows of* **Roy** *and* **Philip** *are lengthening across the field.*

Granddad fancies Harriet. I could tell by the way he asked her for a fried egg.

Philip *is looking at* **Roy**.

I'm not gay, by the way.

Philip   I know.

Roy   I wish I was, Philip. There are no girls round here apart from your mother and Harriet and I don't really fancy them at all.

Roy *is looking at* **Philip**.

Harriet's all right.

Philip *gathers strength.*

Philip Roy, you know your mother is dead.

Roy Yes.

Philip She murdered someone. She drank a canister of weed killer in Twickenham. She went to find James, but he was here.

Roy I know.

Philip It was really, really worrying me. I didn't know whether to tell you or not.

Roy A bit like the Viking?

Philip Yes.

Roy *takes two handfuls of pills from his pockets.*

Roy I've got enough paracetamol to sink a battleship.

Philip Are you going to take them?

Roy I know absolutely everything about you. You know absolutely everything about me. Why ask?

Roy *rubs his hands together so that the pills become dust. A bird comes to life and slowly takes wing into the air. It flies off.*

Did you see it go?

Philip Yes. Fantastic.

Roy *and* **Philip** *see* **Karl** *wandering across the field.*
Karl's *jacket is too small and marked with the yellow Star of David. His clothes are poor quality. His watch is identical to* **Philip**'s *watch. He sees a stray head of wheat. He runs to it and picks it up. He looks at* **Philip** *and* **Roy**. *He puts the wheat back on the ground.*

Take it.

Karl *picks up the wheat. He runs it run through his fingers so that the corn comes into his hand.*

Karl I would make bread with this.

Karl *puts the wheat in his jacket pocket.*

When the schools were finally closed, I went scavenging in the countryside around Berlin.

He sees another head of wheat. He runs to it and picks it up.

I did everything to escape the factories of death. You could die in a moment and not know why.

He runs the wheat through his fingers.

I was innocent, or so I thought.

He puts the corn in his pocket.

At night I would creep back into Berlin, in the shadows, in the dark, where my father was worrying about me.

He runs to another head of corn and picks it up. He looks at **Philip**.

Your grandmother is beautiful.

He runs the wheat through his fingers. He puts the corn in his pocket.

There is a guard in Buchenwald who feeds one child but lets the rest die. It is, of course, our guilt that makes us human.

He takes a step or two towards **Roy** *and* **Philip**.

Your grandfather will tell me that when he learns of these places, it will feel like the end of time. He will say humanity ended there. He will say we have become ghosts for ever. He will be wrong. Buchenwald is not an abomination. It is not a monstrosity. The huts are filled with the kinds of cruelty that people do to each other. It is the kind of thing that always seems to have happened, one way or another.

He takes a step or two towards **Roy** *and* **Philip**.

I must ask you both for your forgiveness. I will put a curse on your family, Philip. You will hear your grandmother say so.

Philip *nods.*

Philip   Yes.

A slight pause.

Karl   History is meaningless. History is out of control. Is any of this important now?

Roy   If it's not important, why do you ask us to forgive you?

Karl   I am really asking you to forgive yourselves, since you cannot have one without the other.

Karl *looks at* **Roy**.

Roy. What about you?

Roy   It's not my family.

Karl   It is your family.

Roy   I know.

A slight pause.

I don't want to forgive you.

Karl   What about you, Philip?

A slight pause.

Philip   I don't want to forgive you either.

One by one all of the dead birds take wing and fly off, astonishing **Philip** *and* **Roy**.

Scene Fifteen

The top field at Mill Farm.
In a few minutes time the world will come to an end. There is a dry stone wall. There is a full moon. The air is clear. The sky is filled with stars and planets. The heavens dominate the earth.
Margaret *is alone. She is looking down over the farm and the fields. She looks up at the sky. Her eyes scan the galaxies.*

Jake *comes on. He stops. He looks at his mother.* **Margaret** *looks at her now oldest son.*
James *comes on. He stops. He has a wooden box.* **Margaret** *turns her head to look at her second oldest son.* **James** *puts the box on the ground. He looks at his mother.*
Philip *comes on. He stops. He is wearing the scarf* **James** *gave him in Exeter.* **Margaret** *turns her head to look at her youngest son. She turns her head and looks at her three children. She looks at the sky.*

Margaret   I was counting the stars. I got to a thousand out of an infinite number.

Edward *comes on. He has a penny-farthing. He stops. He is wearing shorts. His leg is completely healed. He has a bottle of whisky.* **Margaret** *turns her head to look at her third oldest son. A pause.*
Philip *sees something on the ground. He runs and picks it up.*

Philip   Look, Mum.

Margaret   What?

Philip   A snail. Hello, Mr Snail. What do you make of all this in the snail world?

James   Put it down, for goodness' sake.

Philip   We're having a snail party. We've got snail drugs and snail beer and we're going to dance to snail music. There'll be snail boys and everything.

Philip *puts the snail gently on the ground. He stands up and stamps on it.*

James   That was cruel.

Philip   You said put it down.

James   I meant let it go.

Philip   It didn't want to come anyway.

Jake   When will you grow up, Philip?

Philip *looks at his brother* **Jake**.

Philip   Never.

Margaret *looks at her son.*

Margaret   Edward.

Edward   Yes.

Margaret   You always did just come and go. You always did just pack your bags. You were always a surprise for all of us, like this very minute.

Edward   Was I?

A slight pause.

I've no bags this time. I walked from London up the A1 towards Peterborough. There was nobody on the entire road. There were just a lot of abandoned, empty cars. At Little Barford I came across a Ford Fiesta, full of petrol, doors open. A man dead inside. The gear box finally packed in at Nunthorpe. I saw this and thought what the hell. The last mile and a half on a penny-farthing. I've been travelling all day. Hello, Mum.

A slight pause.
Philip *takes a snail from his pocket. He puts it on the palm of his hand.*

Philip   How many acts of cruelty does it take to produce one kindness, Mr Snail?

Philip *looks at his mother.*

Margaret   Hello, Edward.

Edward *holds out the whisky.*

Edward   There was a bottle of whisky in the car.

Margaret *turns her head.*

Margaret   You were wrong, James. You didn't lie after all.

James   William died yesterday.

Edward   I'm sorry.

A slight pause.
Philip *pushes the snail around his palm. He does a snail voice.*

Philip   I think it takes two acts of cruelty, Philip.

Philip *puts the snail on the ground. He moves his leg to stamp on it.*
Margaret *unleashes anger.*

Margaret   Stop it, Philip.

Philip *stops.*
Roy *comes on. He goes towards* **Edward**.

Roy   Can I have a go?

Edward   Yes, if you want to.

Roy   How do you get up?

Edward   Well, you sort of climb up.

Roy   I'll have a go later.

Roy *wheels the penny-farthing towards* **Philip**. *He runs the metal wheels over the snail.*

I'm sorry about crushing you to pulp, Mr. Snail. It's just we're the cruel ones.

Roy *looks up.*

You should all feel better now. You're better than us.

A slight pause.
Harriet *comes on. She goes to* **James**. *She runs her hand down the small of his back. They kiss for a moment.* **Harriet** *goes away to the stone wall.*

Harriet   You can see the sea.

James   Yes.

Harriet   How far is it?

James *joins his wife.*

James   It's about two miles away.

Harriet   It looks like it's boiling up. It looks like it's bubbling. It looks orange. The horses are all still wide awake.

She looks at **James**.

Did you see that?

James   Yes, I definitely did.

Harriet   Is it happening, do you think?

James   I think it's starting.

A slight pause.
Roy *whispers in* **Philip**'s *ear.*

Philip   Mum.

Roy *whispers.*

Roy   Then who?

Philip   James.

Roy   Then who?

Philip   Edward.

Roy   Then who?

Philip   Your granddad.

A slight pause.

Margaret   What did you ask him, Roy?

Roy   I asked him which of you felt most cruel. I asked him which of you felt most guilty. I asked him which of you felt most frightened.

Philip *whispers in* **Roy**'s *ear.*

He asked me, in these final moments on earth, whether I thought you were prepared to forgive yourself, in order to forgive your sons.

Philip *whispers, briefly, in* **Roy**'s *ear.*

He said it's the same for his brothers.

Roy *looks at* **James**.

A little bit of humility wouldn't be amiss, James.

Roy *looks at* **Edward**.

A little bit less self-pity from you, Edward. He knows all about you. Don't worry, he hasn't told anybody.

He looks at his granddad.

Granddad, you escape his vicious tongue for the moment.

Margaret *gathers strength.*

Margaret   Edward.

Edward *gathers strength.*

Edward   Hello.

Margaret   You're here.

Edward   Yes. Hello, Mum.

He looks at **Jake**.

Hello, Jake.

Jake   Edward.

Edward *looks at* **James**.

Edward   James. We met in Euston Square ten days ago.

James   Yes.

Edward   Philip. I've not seen you since you were a baby.

Philip   No.

A slight pause.

Harriet   I'm Harriet, I'm James's wife.

Edward   Hello, Harriet. How lovely to meet you.

Harriet   It's lovely to meet you, too.

Harriet *and* **Edward** *kiss on both cheeks.*

Roy   I'm Roy.

Edward   I thought you would be. I'm Edward.

Roy   Hello.

Roy *and* **Edward** *shake hands.*
Edward *looks at them all.*

Edward   I thought the top field was the place to come.

Edward *looks at his mother.*

Have you seen the sky, Mum?

They look up at the sky.

Margaret   It's rather beautiful, though, I think.

Edward   I do, too.

Roy *leans the penny-farthing against the stone wall.*

Harriet   Is anybody hungry?

Roy   I could eat a horse.

James *picks up the wooden box.*

James   We've brought some cheese. It's kind of my little tribute to William. There's a large piece of Manchego. And some quince jams.

James *puts the box down. The sides have hinges. He unhooks the clasps and lets the sides down to produce a cheese board. He begins to open three small jars of quince jam.*
Roy *cuts himself a piece of cheese.*
Philip *cuts himself a piece of cheese.*
Roy *goes to the wall with a knife and a jar of quince jam. He sits.*
Philip *joins him on the wall. He shares the jam.*
The two boys eat.

Mum.

Margaret   You first.

James   Edward.

Edward *puts the bottle of whisky on the wall. He cuts himself a piece of cheese.*

Jake.

Jake *cuts himself a piece of cheese.*

Harriet.

Harriet *cuts herself a piece of cheese.*
Edward *takes some quince jam from the jar on the wall.*
Jake *picks up a jar of quince jam. He puts some on his cheese with a knife.*
Harriet *takes some quince jam from **Jake**'s jar.*
James *cut himself a piece of cheese. He takes some quince jam from the third jar.*
Margaret *cuts herself a piece of cheese.*
Edward *picks up the jar of quince jam on the wall.*

Edward   Use this one, Mum.

Margaret *goes to **Edward**.*
Edward *spreads some quince jam on his mother's cheese.*
Harriet *sits.*
James *sits.*
They are all eating cheese and quince jam.
Jake *is looking at the sky.*

Margaret   Why did you and William fall out, Jake? I've never understood it. You were so close when you were boys. Please tell me.

Jake *looks at his mother.*

Jake   Not long before he went off to Cirencester, I woke in the night and William was in my bed. I don't think he meant anything by it. He always was a sleepwalker. I suppose he was embarrassed. After that his attitude changed towards me. He crashed the car on purpose.

Roy   Knock knock, granddad.

A slight pause.

James   William remembers it, except he remembers it being in Cirencester.

Jake   No, it was definitely here.

James   Are you sure?

Jake   Yes, it was definitely here at Mill Farm.

Margaret   You all shared beds when you were little. Why should it matter?

Jake   He was deeply ashamed because he had a full erection.

Edward *looks at Jake.*

Edward   Why? Did you kiss him?

Edward *giggles. They all giggle for a moment.*
Roy *jumps down off the wall.*

Roy   Is this Spanish?

James   Yes.

Roy   It's delicious.

Margaret   Did you bring it all the way from Twickenham?

James   Yes.

Roy *cuts himself a piece of cheese. He cuts a piece for* **Philip***. He goes back to the wall.*
Philip *and* **Roy** *share the quince jam.*

Margaret   Was William gay, Philip?

Philip   No.

Jake *goes to the cheese. He sits down.*

Jake   Would anyone like to share this last piece?

Harriet   Yes, please.

Jake *cuts the cheese in two. He gives half to* **Harriet**. *They eat the cheese with quince jam.*

Roy   I wonder what they're doing in Spain at this precise second.

Jake   They're eating Stilton, Roy.

Philip   Cheddar.

Roy   And locally produced Wensleydale with crackers, from Wensleydale sheep. They really are.

They giggle for a moment.

James   French monks brought over cheese-making to the north east in the twelfth century. But their first monastery was grim and their flock was vulnerable to attack from wolves. So, after ten years, they moved and founded Jervaulx Abbey further east. The monks were very rich and trained horses for Henry VIII. Not that he thanked them for it. They took part in a Catholic rebellion and the last Abbot was executed at Tyburn. Then two years later the dissolution of the monasteries took place and four hundred years of history came to an abrupt end.

A slight pause.
Edward *goes to the wall. He takes the bottle of whisky. He unscrews the top. He offers the whisky to* **Jake**.

Jake   No thanks, Edward. Whatever it is, I want to experience it.

Jake *gets up. He walks away a short distance. He stops. He looks at the horizon and the sky.*

Edward   Philip.

Philip   No, thank you.

Edward   James.

James   No, thank you.

James *gets up.*
Harriet *gets up.*
James *squeezes* **Harriet**'s *hand. He walks away a short distance until he is closer to* **Jake**.
He looks at the horizon and the sky.

Edward Harriet.

Harriet No thank you, Edward.

Harriet *takes a step towards* **James**. *She stops. She looks at the horizon and the sky.*

Edward Mum.

Margaret No thank you, sweetheart.

Margaret *looks at the horizon and the sky.*

Edward Roy.

Roy No thanks.

Edward *screws the top on the bottle of whisky. He puts it on the ground. He moves closer to* **Jake** *and* **James**. *He looks at the horizon and the sky.*
A slight pause.
Roy *gets up and stands on the wall.* **Philip** *gets down off the wall. He joins his brothers.*

Philip Does anybody agree with me? The surprising thing is the silence.

Philip *looks up. The stars begin to explode in the sky. It becomes incredibly bright, and then suddenly the whole world is black.*

The end.

Methuen Drama Student Editions

Jean Anouilh *Antigone* • John Arden *Serjeant Musgrave's Dance* Alan Ayckbourn *Confusions* • Aphra Behn *The Rover* • Edward Bond *Lear* • *Saved* • Bertolt Brecht *The Caucasian Chalk Circle* • *Fear and Misery in the Third Reich* • *The Good Person of Szechwan* • *Life of Galileo* • *Mother Courage and her Children* • *The Resistible Rise of Arturo Ui* • *The Threepenny Opera* • Anton Chekhov *The Cherry Orchard* • *The Seagull* • *Three Sisters* • *Uncle Vanya* • Caryl Churchill *Serious Money* • *Top Girls* • Shelagh Delaney *A Taste of Honey* • Euripides *Elektra* • *Medea* • Dario Fo *Accidental Death of an Anarchist* • Michael Frayn *Copenhagen* • John Galsworthy *Strife* • Nikolai Gogol *The Government Inspector* • Robert Holman *Across Oka* • Henrik Ibsen *A Doll's House* • *Ghosts* • *Hedda Gabler* • Charlotte Keatley *My Mother Said I Never Should* • Bernard Kops *Dreams of Anne Frank* • Federico García Lorca *Blood Wedding* • *Doña Rosita the Spinster* (bilingual edition) • *The House of Bernarda Alba* • (bilingual edition) • *Yerma* (bilingual edition) • David Mamet *Glengarry Glen Ross* • *Oleanna* • Patrick Marber *Closer* • John Marston *Malcontent* • Martin McDonagh *The Lieutenant of Inishmore* • Joe Orton *Loot* • Luigi Pirandello *Six Characters in Search of an Author* • Mark Ravenhill *Shopping and F***ing* • Willy Russell *Blood Brothers* • *Educating Rita* • Sophocles *Antigone* • *Oedipus the King* • Wole Soyinka *Death and the King's Horseman* • Shelagh Stephenson *The Memory of Water* • August Strindberg *Miss Julie* • J. M. Synge *The Playboy of the Western World* • Theatre Workshop *Oh What a Lovely War* Timberlake Wertenbaker *Our Country's Good* • Arnold Wesker *The Merchant* • Oscar Wilde *The Importance of Being Earnest* • Tennessee Williams *A Streetcar Named Desire* • *The Glass Menagerie*

Methuen Drama Modern Plays

include work by

Edward Albee
Jean Anouilh
John Arden
Margaretta D'Arcy
Peter Barnes
Sebastian Barry
Brendan Behan
Dermot Bolger
Edward Bond
Bertolt Brecht
Howard Brenton
Anthony Burgess
Simon Burke
Jim Cartwright
Caryl Churchill
Complicite
Noël Coward
Lucinda Coxon
Sarah Daniels
Nick Darke
Nick Dear
Shelagh Delaney
David Edgar
David Eldridge
Dario Fo
Michael Frayn
John Godber
Paul Godfrey
David Greig
John Guare
Peter Handke
David Harrower
Jonathan Harvey
Iain Heggie
Declan Hughes
Terry Johnson
Sarah Kane
Charlotte Keatley
Barrie Keeffe

Howard Korder
Robert Lepage
Doug Lucie
Martin McDonagh
John McGrath
Terrence McNally
David Mamet
Patrick Marber
Arthur Miller
Mtwa, Ngema & Simon
Tom Murphy
Phyllis Nagy
Peter Nichols
Sean O'Brien
Joseph O'Connor
Joe Orton
Louise Page
Joe Penhall
Luigi Pirandello
Stephen Poliakoff
Franca Rame
Mark Ravenhill
Philip Ridley
Reginald Rose
Willy Russell
Jean-Paul Sartre
Sam Shepard
Wole Soyinka
Simon Stephens
Shelagh Stephenson
Peter Straughan
C. P. Taylor
Theatre Workshop
Sue Townsend
Judy Upton
Timberlake Wertenbaker
Roy Williams
Snoo Wilson
Victoria Wood

Methuen Drama Modern Classics

Jean Anouilh *Antigone* • Brendan Behan *The Hostage* • Robert Bolt *A Man for All Seasons* • Edward Bond *Saved* • Bertolt Brecht *The Caucasian Chalk Circle* • *Fear and Misery in the Third Reich* • *The Good Person of Szechwan* • *Life of Galileo* • *The Messingkauf Dialogues* • *Mother Courage and Her Children* • *Mr Puntila and His Man Matti* • *The Resistible Rise of Arturo Ui* • *Rise and Fall of the City of Mahagonny* • *The Threepenny Opera* • Jim Cartwright *Road* • *Two & Bed* • Caryl Churchill *Serious Money* • *Top Girls* • Noël Coward *Blithe Spirit* • *Hay Fever* • *Present Laughter* • *Private Lives* • *The Vortex* • Shelagh Delaney *A Taste of Honey* • Dario Fo *Accidental Death of an Anarchist* • Michael Frayn *Copenhagen* • Lorraine Hansberry *A Raisin in the Sun* • Jonathan Harvey *Beautiful Thing* • David Mamet *Glengarry Glen Ross* • *Oleanna* • *Speed-the-Plow* • Patrick Marber *Closer* • *Dealer's Choice* • Arthur Miller *Broken Glass* • Percy Mtwa, Mbongeni Ngema, Barney Simon *Woza Albert!* • Joe Orton *Entertaining Mr Sloane* • *Loot* • *What the Butler Saw* • Mark Ravenhill *Shopping and F***ing* • Willy Russell *Blood Brothers* • *Educating Rita* • *Stags and Hens* • *Our Day Out* • Jean-Paul Sartre *Crime Passionnel* • Wole Soyinka • *Death and the King's Horseman* • Theatre Workshop *Oh, What a Lovely War* • Frank Wedekind • *Spring Awakening* • Timberlake Wertenbaker *Our Country's Good*

Methuen Drama Contemporary Dramatists

include

John Arden (two volumes)
Arden & D'Arcy
Peter Barnes (three volumes)
Sebastian Barry
Dermot Bolger
Edward Bond (eight volumes)
Howard Brenton
(two volumes)
Richard Cameron
Jim Cartwright
Caryl Churchill (two volumes)
Sarah Daniels (two volumes)
Nick Darke
David Edgar (three volumes)
David Eldridge
Ben Elton
Dario Fo (two volumes)
Michael Frayn (three volumes)
David Greig
John Godber (four volumes)
Paul Godfrey
John Guare
Lee Hall (two volumes)
Peter Handke
Jonathan Harvey
(two volumes)
Declan Hughes
Terry Johnson (three volumes)
Sarah Kane
Barrie Keeffe
Bernard-Marie Koltès
(two volumes)
Franz Xaver Kroetz
David Lan
Bryony Lavery
Deborah Levy
Doug Lucie

David Mamet (four volumes)
Martin McDonagh
Duncan McLean
Anthony Minghella
(two volumes)
Tom Murphy (six volumes)
Phyllis Nagy
Anthony Neilsen (two volumes)
Philip Osment
Gary Owen
Louise Page
Stewart Parker (two volumes)
Joe Penhall (two volumes)
Stephen Poliakoff
(three volumes)
David Rabe (two volumes)
Mark Ravenhill (two volumes)
Christina Reid
Philip Ridley
Willy Russell
Eric-Emmanuel Schmitt
Ntozake Shange
Sam Shepard (two volumes)
Wole Soyinka (two volumes)
Simon Stephens (two volumes)
Shelagh Stephenson
David Storey (three volumes)
Sue Townsend
Judy Upton
Michel Vinaver
(two volumes)
Arnold Wesker (two volumes)
Michael Wilcox
Roy Williams (three volumes)
Snoo Wilson (two volumes)
David Wood (two volumes)
Victoria Wood

Methuen Drama Classical Greek Dramatists

Aeschylus Plays: One
(Persians, Seven Against Thebes, Suppliants,
Prometheus Bound)

Aeschylus Plays: Two
(Oresteia: Agamemnon, Libation-Bearers, Eumenides)

Aristophanes Plays: One
(Acharnians, Knights, Peace, Lysistrata)

Aristophanes Plays: Two
(Wasps, Clouds, Birds, Festival Time, Frogs)

Aristophanes & Menander: New Comedy
(Women in Power, Wealth, The Malcontent,
The Woman from Samos)

Euripides Plays: One
(Medea, The Phoenician Women, Bacchae)

Euripides Plays: Two
(Hecuba, The Women of Troy, Iphigeneia at Aulis,
Cyclops)

Euripides Plays: Three
(Alkestis, Helen, Ion)

Euripides Plays: Four
(Elektra, Orestes, Iphigeneia in Tauris)

Euripides Plays: Five
(Andromache, Herakles' Children, Herakles)

Euripides Plays: Six
(Hippolytos, Suppliants, Rhesos)

Sophocles Plays: One
(Oedipus the King, Oedipus at Colonus, Antigone)

Sophocles Plays: Two
(Ajax, Women of Trachis, Electra, Philoctetes)

UNIVERSITY OF WINCHESTER
LIBRARY